MARYLAND'S CHESAPEAKE

How the Bay and Its Bounty Shaped a Cuisine

KATHY WIELECH PATTERSON and NEAL PATTERSON

MARYLAND'S CHESAPEAKE

How the Bay and Its Bounty Shaped a Cuisine

KATHY WIELECH PATTERSON and NEAL PATTERSON

Globe
Pequot

Guilford, Connecticut

Globe
Pequot

An imprint of Rowman & Littlefield
Distributed by NATIONAL BOOK NETWORK

Copyright © 2016 Rowman & Littlefield

British Library Cataloguing in Publication Information Available
Library of Congress Cataloging-in-Publication Data Available

ISBN 978-1-4930-1791-1 (paperback)
ISBN 978-1-4930-1792-8 (e-book)

∞™ The paper used in this publication meets the minimum requirements of American National Standard for Information Sciences—Permanence of Paper for Printed Library Materials, ANSI/NISO Z39.48-1992.

Contents

Acknowledgments

This is our third book for Globe Pequot and we want to start off by thanking them for having faith in our ability to talk knowledgeably about food, more specifically, the food of the great state of Maryland. Our gratitude to everyone there who helped with this project.

A big shout out to Maryland photographer Jay Fleming for allowing us to use several of his fabulous photos of the Chesapeake Bay, its denizens, and the people who work with them. We are in awe of his work; you can see more in his book, *Working the Water*. Also check out his website at JayFlemingPhotography.com. We'd also like to thank the lovely and talented Frances Burman, Melinda Cordero, Tim Devine, and Jessica Lemmo for additional photography. Thanks to Jay Hood, too, for the excellent camera recommendation, without which our food photos wouldn't look nearly as good.

Many thanks to fish god Steve Vilnit for taking the time to answer our many, possibly annoying, Bay-related questions, and for fact-checking several chapters to make sure we didn't say anything dumb. Also thanks to Paul Schurick of the Oyster Recovery Partnership for the same, but in an oyster vein. We're grateful for any and all info provided by Tom Zolper and John Surrick of the Chesapeake Bay Foundation, Vanessa Orlando from the Maryland Department of Agriculture, Dale Hawks from the USDA National Agricultural Statistics Service, and Dr. Standish Allen from the Virginia Institute of Marine Science.

A great big thanks to Tim Devine from Barren Island Oysters, Jaime Windon & Ben Lyon of Lyon Distillery, and Dr Yonathan Zohar from the Aquaculture Research Center of the Institute of Marine and Environmental Technology at UMBC, for giving us insight into the future of three of the Chesapeake Bay area's most delicious food and beverage products.

Thanks also to Wanda Cogan, Dara Bunjon, Brian Michael Lawrence, Kit Pollard, Austin Murphy, and Jessica Oring, for helpful suggestions and stuff like press passes and recipe-wrangling skills. *Merci beaucoup* to our dear friend Kate Becker for moral support and a very helpful read-through of the manuscript.

Most of all, we'd like to offer sincere thanks to all of the Chesapeake Bay Watershed–area chefs who agreed to create dishes and donate recipes

Thinkstock

and photos for this project: Don Applebaum and Kate Applebaum of Cajun Kate's; Winston Blick of Clementine; Michael Ransom, Scott Hines, and Brendan Dorr of B&O American Brasserie; Annmarie Langton of the Gypsy Queen Café food trucks; Keith Long of Harvest Wood Grill + Tap; Chris Vocci from Alexandra's of Turf Valley; Zack Mills from Wit & Wisdom; Cyrus Keefer from the Baltimore Country Club; Adam Snyder from Brew House No. 16; pastry guru Bettina Perry; and most especially, Chad Wells from Alewife. Without their help, we wouldn't have been able to put together such a great selection of classic and modern Maryland recipes inspired by the Chesapeake Bay.

About the Authors

Kathy Wielech Patterson has written everything from auction catalogs to fine jewelry appraisals to reports on social welfare issues. It wasn't until she started the food blog, Minxeats.com, that she realized she most loved writing about food. In addition to blogging, Kathy has also written for *Baltimore Magazine* and *Food Republic*.

Neal Patterson, for many years a writer in the financial industry, is primarily a fiction writer. He's contributed to the anthologies *The Dead Walk!* and *Hey Kids, Comics!*, and the website, Channel 37: Serial Science Fiction from the Distant Reaches of UHF. He's also the author of *The Codename: Carla Casebook*, published in 2014.

Together, the Pattersons are known as the Baltimore Dining Duo and have written for local magazines *Discover Baltimore* and *Towson Life*. They are the authors of *Food Lovers' Guide to Baltimore* (Globe Pequot, 2013), and *Baltimore Chef's Table* (Globe Pequot, 2014).

© Frances Burman

Chef Biographies

Don and Kate Applebaum

Despite being a Philly boy, Don Applebaum makes the best gumbo ever. Seriously. We ate it in New Orleans sixteen years ago and have been making pilgrimages to buy it at his Boothwyn, Pennsylvania, food stand, Cajun Kate's, for years now. Don and wife Kate both graduated from the Restaurant School at Walnut Hill College in Philadelphia, and then moved to New Orleans. There, Don cooked for Emeril Lagasse before coming home to open his own, award-winning, Cajun place. Kate, a well-rounded chef who isn't afraid of pastry, worked for Susan Spicer at Bayona in the city's French Quarter, and was most recently the chef de cuisine at Harry's Seafood Grill in Wilmington, Delaware.

Winston Blick

Nineteenth-century Shady Side, Maryland, waterman Captain Salem Avery was one of Chef Winston Blick's forebears; his home is now a museum. Blick's "home" is Clementine, a Baltimore-area catering company that he owns with his amazing wife Cristin Dadant. Winston and company produce the best charcuterie in town, even seafood versions, and a coconut cake to die for. With both crabbers and oystermen in his family, Blick's got shellfish in his blood, and one will often find one or both of these ingredients on his menus, along with anything else that is seasonal, locally produced, and completely delicious.

Brendan Dorr

Brendan Dorr is the founder of the Baltimore Bartenders' Guild and head bartender at B&O American Brasserie, a fine place to have a tasty libation or three. We've tried many of Brendan's drinks over the years and marvel at his creativity. The mustachioed mixologist supreme gets his ideas from all over, "from the food I eat to the seasons of the year. Sometimes from classic recipes, sometimes from new or contemporary ones." He's a big proponent of studying the basics, and his knowledge of old cocktails like Sazeracs and French 75s informs his ability to create concoctions that may someday become new classics.

© Jay Fleming

Scott Hines

Scott Hines—a generous man and the rare chef who responds quickly to emails!—is from Harleysville in the Chesapeake Bay watershed state of Pennsylvania. Though his father was also a chef, Hines hadn't originally intended to follow the same career path. Nevertheless, after realizing he both enjoyed cooking and was pretty good at it, he attended Stratford University for a few semesters and learned the rest on the job. A fan of using Chesapeake Bay-area products in season, Hines worked at notable local restaurants Wit & Wisdom, Pabu, the Wine Market, Heavy Seas Ale House, and Farmstead Grill before his current position at B&O American Brasserie.

Cyrus Keefer

Delaware native Cyrus Keefer originally wanted to be a rock star. Despite plying his trade in the kitchen instead of on stage, he has achieved his goal. Keefer recently participated in his third dinner at the James Beard House in New York City, working with other Baltimore-area chefs to celebrate the cuisine of the Chesapeake Bay region. That's what we call a rock star! A graduate of Philadelphia's Restaurant School at Walnut Hill College, Keefer is currently working his magic at the Baltimore Country Club. He's also got several restaurant concepts spinning around in his head and we can't wait until he opens one or all of them.

Keith Long

Keith Long, executive chef at Harvest Wood Grill + Tap in Annapolis, was born in Texas but raised in Annapolis. This lifelong exposure to the bounty of the Chesapeake Bay has made seafood his favorite thing to cook, to the good fortune of Marylanders. His cuisine is bold and creative, and while he's not afraid of using the occasional modernist technique (liquid nitrogen ice cream, anyone?), Long always shows the utmost respect for the ingredients he works with. "I love the history behind classic dishes, and while honoring the past I like to put my own twist on something to make the familiar unexpected."

Annmarie Langton

Annmarie Langton has always been in the kitchen. She was born in the leftmost compartment of a three-compartment sink, won her first cooking competition at the tender age of fourteen, then quickly worked her way up to executive chef at Opa! and Helen's Garden, both in Baltimore. Langton is a partner in the multi-award-winning Gypsy Queen Café food trucks, where she serves her crab cakes in waffle cones. When she's not appearing on cooking shows involving competitions, tacos, and Aaron Sanchez, Annmarie lives in Roland Park, with her dog, Jack. She is open to human companionship as well, as long as he's not needy.

Zack Mills

A graduate of the French Culinary Institute in New York, Zack Mills worked at Michael Mina's award-winning Bourbon Steak DC before becoming a corporate chef for the Mina Group. Today, he's the executive chef at Mina's Wit & Wisdom in the Four Seasons Baltimore. A native Marylander, Mills is a culinary artist who possesses both a wealth of knowledge about the cuisine of the Chesapeake Bay area and a love for using local ingredients. It's no coincidence that the best sellers on his menu at Wit & Wisdom are the Maryland Crab Tasting (a "greatest hits" sampler of blue crab preparations) and any dish using local rockfish. Both are "synonymous with our area and dishes that we developed to showcase the state's amazing seafood offerings."

Bettina Perry

Currently a freelancer, Bettina Perry grew up in Napa Valley, where she spent lots of time in the kitchen baking cookies and pies and other naughty things with her mother and grandmothers. While in Baltimore, Perry has worked for the Bagby Group, Bonjour Bakery, Brasserie Tatin, Blue Hill Tavern, and Linwood's. She's received kudos from both local media and StarChefs.com and was named 2010's Best Pastry Chef by *Baltimore Magazine*. She clearly appreciates a challenge, as in the one we gave her, which makes her our very favorite pastry chef, too.

Mike Ransom

Mike Ransom began his appreciation for local ingredients and regional techniques in his youth. Growing up in northern Michigan, he foraged for sumac, morels, and ramps, and cooked maple sap into syrup. With this early experience under his belt, Ransom went to Chicago, where he attended Kendall Culinary College, and then on to work in San Francisco. Today, he's running the kitchen at the B&O American Brasserie in Baltimore, where the relative simplicity of his menu belies the complexity of techniques and flavors in his dishes. Mike's cooking demonstrates his clear respect for the area's freshest seafood and produce, and we're hoping he makes Baltimore his permanent home.

Adam Snyder

Baltimore-born Adam Snyder was raised in York County, Pennsylvania, after a detour through California, places that instilled an appreciation for fresh food and the hard-working yet laid-back farming way of life. He graduated from Baltimore International College and spent time in Pittsburgh and New York before coming back to his birthplace. There Adam did the corporate chef thing at Phillip's, Paolo's, and McCormick & Schmick. He also worked at Cunningham's before landing his current position as executive chef at Brew House No. 16, a challenging but creatively fulfilling position where he sources his own ingredients and cooks them as his passion dictates.

Chris Vocci

Chef Vocci was born in Baltimore but raised in Montgomery County, Maryland. He spent some formative years on Maryland's Eastern Shore while attending Salisbury University, where social events revolved around "shucking corn, making tomato salads, and enjoying a bushel of crabs as often as possible." After honing his cooking chops at the Baltimore International College, he cooked here and there around the area before landing the job of executive chef for Alexandra's Restaurant at Turf Valley in Ellicott City, Maryland, a destination for many out-of-town visitors. There, he takes pride in showcasing what makes the Chesapeake region a special place, with a strong focus on local seafood and produce.

Chad Wells

Chad Wells might be considered a fisherman first, chef second. The Ellicott City native is passionate about the Chesapeake and its products and is especially eager to eradicate the destructive invasive species, like snakehead and blue catfish, which have infested local rivers. To this end, he's appeared on the Cooking Channel's *Hook, Line & Dinner*. "I love fishing. And if I can use it to benefit everyone around us, it's awesome." Currently, he's the executive chef at Alewife, in Baltimore City, where you'll find both sophisticated cooking and dishes that make perfect accompaniments to copious beer drinking, not to mention one of the best crab cakes around.

Introduction

Quick story:

A few years back a friend of ours from North Carolina was in Baltimore for a seminar at Johns Hopkins University. During her brief free time, we wanted to give her a crash course in some of Baltimore's unique qualities. One of those must-have experiences was a crab feast. After picking our friend up at her hotel, we drove over to a crab shack on Greenmount Avenue where we could get a half-bushel of crabs for about $75. The air was swimming with the familiar odors of a fish market, and refrigerator cases were brimming with piles of crabs, shrimp, and other varieties of seafood. The floor was slightly wet from melting ice. Our friend seemed a bit apprehensive and dubious about our dinner choice. After picking up our boxes filled with steamed sea creatures, we drove to our house where some family members were waiting to rip those critters apart.

With mallets and knives in hand, we explained the procedure for properly stripping a crab of its delicious flesh. Rip off the claws, crack them open and suck out the meat, peel back the apron on the underbelly, and so forth. Our visitor followed along like a trouper and started to take apart a few crabs. Meanwhile, the rest of us were already bashing and cracking away at the hard shells, relishing every morsel of white meat we could extract from the carcasses. The crabs were on the small side, but with a half-bushel (about four dozen crabs), there were plenty to go around. After three crabs, our friend politely gave up and shifted her attention to some corn on the cob.

As she watched us plow through the crabs and a mountain of carapace formed in the center of our dining room table, I couldn't help but sense her bewilderment. We must have appeared to her like a tribe disemboweling a feral pig on the plains of Namibia. By the end of the evening, we felt a bit guilty. She certainly could not have had enough to eat and the experience was probably more head scratching than gratifying. While the crab feast is a saliva-inducing ritual of avaricious anticipation for native Marylanders, perhaps to outsiders it's just a tedious slog for a little bit of protein. Marylanders, however, are conditioned from birth to crave that sweet, fluffy protein and will put in whatever cracking, smashing, digging, and slurping is necessary to get our fill.

The crab feast is a typical example of the singular fixations Marylanders have with their cuisine. We crave all things made with blue crab: steamed crabs, crab soup, crab imperial, crab dip. We love oysters and rockfish. We can't wait until the sweet white corn and juicy tomatoes grown on the Eastern Shore begin to pop up at roadside produce stands during the summer. More than any particular cuisine, it's the ingredients themselves that define how we eat, and all those ingredients are thanks to the Chesapeake Bay.

Since prehistoric times, the Bay has sustained and fortified those who lived along its shores. Native Americans built their whole tribal culture around the cyclical nature of breeding habits and growing seasons. When the colonists came from England, they saw a land of great bounty ready to be exploited. Not only was there seafood and crops to consume, there was tobacco to smoke and trees with which to build boats. An estuary of the Susquehanna River to the north and a gateway to the Atlantic Ocean to the

© Thinkstock

south, trade routes were wide open for those who settled by the Bay. The Industrial Revolution brought railroads connecting Maryland to the western United States, making cities like Baltimore thriving economic hubs.

Of course, all good things come with a price, and the exuberant exploitation of the Bay has taken its toll. The Eastern Shore suffered catastrophic deforestation in the 1800s. Numerous forms of fish and mollusks have been fished into extinction or near-extinction. What hasn't been killed by overfishing is threatened by pollution that runs off from factories, farms, and even residential properties. It has shown tremendous resilience over the centuries, but a constant struggle continues to preserve the delicate balance of the ecosystem while still providing the seafood, produce, and poultry we crave.

In the following pages, we hope to take you through all the changes the Chesapeake Bay has gone through and how Marylanders have affected and are affected by this remarkable estuary. In addition to historical information, we've included a selection of recipes that utilize the bounty of the Chesapeake region, from flora to fauna. While we will present many recipes traditionally associated with Maryland, we also have some new receipts that incorporate modern ingredients and techniques. Along the way, we hope to dispel some preconceived notions about Maryland cuisine.

As an example, many people think certain classic Maryland dishes, like crab soup, have only one true version, but that is not the case. For one thing, there are two distinct styles of crab soup served here, the type normally referred to as "Maryland crab soup," and cream of crab. Both styles have multiple variations, most likely created by cooks using ingredients they had on hand. For instance, Maryland crab soup can be made with or without a meat-based stock, and with or without tomatoes. To keep with the spirit of innovation, for many traditional foodstuffs we've included both our favorite "classic" dish along with a modernized version. Many of the new dishes have been created by some of the best chefs working in Maryland today. We encourage you to try both variations, and also to put your own spin on dishes. As long as you're working with delicious Maryland products, the possibilities are nearly endless.

Part 1

A Tale of Two Shores: The Backstory to Maryland's Chesapeake

The former slave turned abolitionist Frederick Douglass saw the Chesapeake Bay as a symbol of freedom. He was born in Talbot County on Maryland's Eastern Shore in 1818 (his exact birthdate is unknown) and was moved from one plantation to another at an early age. While life on the plantation was secluded and isolated, black seamen who worked aboard the ships that ferried goods up and down the Chesapeake were afforded greater freedom and the ability to see new towns and cities. Douglass's cousin Tom worked aboard the sloop *Sally Lloyd*, captained by their master Thomas Auld. The plantation slaves admired the sailor slaves and loved to hear the stories of their travels when they returned home. Douglass knew that, "This very bay shall yet bear me into freedom."

By the early nineteenth century, a dynamic shift had occurred in Maryland's economy. Tobacco, the king crop that had fueled the wealth of Maryland during the seventeenth and eighteenth centuries, was yielding to the booming shipping and fishing businesses. Port cities like Baltimore and Annapolis were gaining prominence, while the largely isolated Eastern Shore was stuck in time. Douglass saw both sides of this dynamic when he was sent to Baltimore to work as a houseboy for Thomas Auld's cousin Hugh. Mrs. Auld was kind to young Douglass, even teaching him how to read. Hugh Auld disapproved since it was illegal in Maryland to teach a slave to read and write, so Mrs. Auld had to stop their lessons. This fueled Douglass's distaste for slavery and his desire to become a free man.

When Douglass was returned to Thomas Auld and Talbot County, his determination increased. Douglass was sent to work for Edward Covey, a poor farmer with a reputation for torturing

his slaves. Temperamental crops like tobacco required constant attention and plantation owners in Maryland could be exceptionally cruel in their methods to keep workers toiling away. Covey tried to break Douglass, but it didn't happen. Douglass eventually left the plantation known as "Mount Misery" and returned to Baltimore where he hatched a plan to find freedom. Dressed as a sailor and borrowing the Seaman's Protection Certificate of a black sailor on liberty, Douglass took a train from the Baltimore neighborhood of Canton to Havre de Grace in northeast Maryland. From there he traveled to Delaware and on to Philadelphia, a free state.

It's unlikely that Frederick Douglass's story could have taken place anywhere else in the United States at that time. Slaves in states farther south had to travel far greater distances and endure greater hardships to reach the faraway free states in the north. Also, plantation life was far more insular and entrenched, discouraging any hope that the African American slaves could ever be free. Maryland and Virginia, on the other hand, experienced a unique evolution driven by the commercial potential of the Chesapeake Bay. These same unique qualities also drove a culinary history based more on the bounty of the bay itself than on the cultures of the people who lived there.

The First Tenants

American history books often make first mention of the Chesapeake Bay in relation to John Smith (c.1580-1631) and the establishment of Jamestown. Captain Christopher Newport (1561-1617) sailed his three ships, *Discovery, Godspeed,* and *Susan Constant* up the Bay in 1607 in search of gold. The legendary John Smith observed the variety of fish and mollusks in the bay as well as the fertile land along its shores and declared, "Heaven and Earth seemed never to agree better to frame a place for man's commodious habitation." But human beings were making good use of the Bay thousands of years before the English arrived.

The massive polar ice floe that covered a large portion of North America during the Ice Age ended just north of the territory that would become the Chesapeake Bay. Paleo-Indians lived in the area around 11000 BC to 9500 BC hunting mammoth and bison. Once the ice began to melt during the Archaic Period (9500 BC–1250 BC), the Susquehanna River and the Chesapeake Bay were carved into the ground by the massive flood of rushing water. Soon, Piscataway and Nanticoke tribes were eating oysters and other seafood from the Bay. As far back as three thousand years ago, these Native American tribes began farming the land along the shores, raising corn and tobacco. By the time the English had arrived, about 24,000 Native Americans of thirty tribes had developed an elaborate and sophisticated system of hunting, fishing, and farming.

Seasonal and sustainable farming may seem like hipster trends today, but for the tribes along the Chesapeake in the seventeenth century, it meant their very survival. Winters found the tribes living in large villages, hunting and gathering whatever food was available. Come spring, the tribes would disperse into smaller groups along the many rivers and tributaries of the bay to fish and hunt small game like raccoons, opossum, and squirrels. Summer meant planting season, so the tribes would gather again to plant fields of corn, beans, tuckahoe (a starchy tuber), and green wheat. They would also enjoy the abundance of fish, oysters, and crabs available during the warmer months. Fall was harvesting time and the season for hunting waterfowl and deer.

It was certainly fortuitous for the English settlers that the Native Americans had perfected their food-gathering skills because the English were pretty hopeless at feeding themselves. As school children, we all learned of the hardships at Jamestown and how John Smith evoked the biblical sentiment, "he that will not work shall not eat." It's not entirely clear why the settlers had so much difficulty provisioning food. Lost supplies, poor choice of land, bad water, and disease were all factors, but part of the problem may have been the character of the settlers themselves.

Unlike the Puritans in New England who set out to establish an agrarian society based on self-sufficiency, the English who came to the Chesapeake shores were fortune hunters and members of the aristocracy. They had no

THE PORTRAICTUER OF CAPTAYNE JOHN SMITH ADMIRALL OF NEW ENGLAND.

© Thinkstock

background in farming and viewed hunting and fishing as merely recreational sports. Maryland's history begins with an aristocrat—the second Lord Baltimore, Cecil Calvert (1605-1675). His family had dreamed of establishing a colony in the new world and, after his father, George Calvert (1579-1631), had to abandon his plans for a settlement in Newfoundland, Cecil Calvert sent his younger brother Leonard (1606-1647) to establish a colony in Maryland.

Coming across on the ships *Ark* and *Dove*, Leonard Calvert set up a colony near the mouth of the Potomac River at St. Clement's Island. Calvert's party landed on March 25, 1634. He named the land Maryland in honor of Charles I's queen and their village St. Mary's City because of their Catholic background. As governor of the new colony, he met with the *tayac*, or leader, of the Piscataway tribe, who granted him permission to settle. The Piscataway soon taught the newcomers how to farm.

The Twin Evils of Tobacco and Slavery

By this time, English settlers in Virginia had already mastered growing the one crop that they couldn't eat: tobacco. The Native Americans had been growing tobacco for recreational purposes for years, but the complicated nature of the growing process had eluded the English until 1622 when John Rolph successfully grew a crop using seed from the West Indies. With tobacco becoming increasingly popular in Europe, the settlers finally had a commodity with which they could make their fortunes.

In little time, a functioning society developed around St. Mary's City as the tobacco trade prospered. With the dual needs of shipping their product and feeding their workers increasing, a community of fishermen, boat builders, and farmers lived and worked in a five-mile area around the city. The success of tobacco farming put a strain on relations between the English and the Indian tribes. Even though the Indians helped the English survive in the early years, once the settlers could grow food themselves and pay to import other needed goods from Europe, they had little use for the original tenants. Conflicts between the settlers and the Native Americans eventually forced the tribes westward. The Chesapeake was now left primarily to the English to exploit. This was good news for the tobacco farmers because, not only was tobacco a difficult and time-consuming crop, it quickly sapped the nutrients of the soil, requiring more and more land. Plantations spread across Maryland to fill the insatiable desire for tobacco in the old country, but this created a new problem.

What is This Chesapeake of Which You Speak?

Throughout this book, we'll be discussing the importance of the Chesapeake Bay, not only from a culinary standpoint, but from the perspective of American history in general. What is it about this body of water that made it so critical to so many people? As they say in the real estate business, the three keys to success are location, location, location.

During the Ice Age, vast expanses of ice one-mile thick covered much of Pennsylvania. When the ice started to melt, rivers and tributaries formed, including what is now the Susquehanna River. This river flooded several times, carving out the parameters of what would become the Chesapeake Bay. At this point, however, a network of river channels wound their way southward toward a single tidal river somewhere along a now-submerged section of the continental shelf. Around 18,000 years ago, what we now know as the modern Chesapeake Bay drainage region formed during the Wisconsin glaciation and the Bay that we see today took shape around 6,000 years later. Some believe that an asteroid hurtling at 50,000 miles per hour toward the earth may have been responsible for the mile-deep, fifty-six-mile-wide crater at the mouth of the bay. All this adds up to the creation of an estuary, or trailing part of a river whose currents meet the sea.

Fresh water from the mountains mixing with the salty ocean currents creates a special breeding ground for shellfish, rockfish, and menhaden. Moreover, the sub-tropical climate of the Mid-Atlantic region gives the Bay one of the widest ranges of annual temperature differences in the world for a coastal ecosystem. These ingredients, along with a neighboring continental shelf, allow boreal, temperate, and subtropical species to thrive in one location.

The Chesapeake Bay extends almost 195 miles, fairly splitting the state of Maryland down the middle and touching the Virginia coast as it empties into the Atlantic Ocean. It's the largest estuary in North America, fed mainly by the Susquehanna and James Rivers. The Potomac, Rappahannock and York Rivers also feed into the bay along its route, providing 90 percent of the Bay's volume with some 50 smaller rivers making up the difference. With 2.5 million cubic feet of freshwater and sediment flowing into the Bay each year, that amounts to 2,500 square miles of surface area with an average water depth of twenty-one feet. Its salinity is near zero at the Susquehanna and 30 parts per 1,000 where it meets the Atlantic Ocean.

The Chesapeake can be broken down into three distinct environmental areas: the Bay, the Coastal Plain, and the Piedmont. The Bay consists of deep and shallow open salt waters and brackish waters of the lower tidal portions of rivers. The Coastal Plain, also called the Tidewater region, borders the Bay and consists of beaches, marshes, forests, and grasslands

0

50km

Susquehanna

Maryland

Gunpowder

Patapsco

Baltimore

Sassafras

Severn

Chester

DELAWARE
BAY

Annapolis

South

Delaware

Potomac

Washington, D.C.

CHESAPEAKE
BAY

Choptank

Nanticoke

Patuxent

Wicomico

Virginia

Rappahannock

CHESAPEAKE
BAY

York

James

ATLANTIC
OCEAN

© Kathy Wielech Patterson

growing on generally sandy or gravelly soils. Land on the eastern and southern shores tends to be flat while the western shore has bluffs and low rolling hills. Farther inland lies the Piedmont, or foothills, a mix of hardwood forests and softwood barren lands bordering on swift running freshwater rivers and streams. Low mountain chains and hills of hard rock resistant to the eroding effects of the water rise above broad valleys covered by clay soil.

Native Americans lived happily for centuries around the Chesapeake Bay, feeding on the diverse and abundant seafood available in the water, hunting game and growing food on the rich and fertile land, and thriving in the mild weather of the sub-tropical climate. Later, the settlers who steered their ships into the mouth of the Chesapeake could not believe their good fortune at finding such an area so hospitable to human habitation. Along with the Puritans in New England, the birth of the United States of America began along the shores of the Chesapeake. No one can resist a prime chunk of real estate.

New and larger plantations required more help to keep them functioning. With hard economic times in England, many plantation owners hired indentured servants. Down-on-their-luck British citizens were willing to go into servitude for a period of seven years in exchange for an opportunity at a fresh start in the New World. Some tobacco growers even imported convicts to work the fields. This strange mix of landed gentry, indentured servants, and convicts working under intense conditions made for a strained environment. As the economy improved in England, fewer people were interested in an Atlantic cruise and seven years of unpaid employment. Reluctantly, the plantation owners turned to importing slaves from West Africa.

Between 1690 and 1770, over 100,000 African slaves were shipped to the Chesapeake shores. The working conditions were particularly brutal given the intense demands of the crop. These conditions also created a closer working relationship between whites and blacks than what existed in the colonies farther south. For example, the whites wanted to keep their slaves healthy and strong so they could work long hours in the fields. Therefore, the whites took it upon themselves to provide food for the slaves rather than have them grow their own. Wealthy owners could afford to have food imported to supplement the local fare. From England came wheat, barley, ale, beef, and vegetable seed. More beef came from New England, Pennsylvania offered dairy products, and rice was imported from North Carolina. Locally grown corn was still a staple and local pork was more common than beef since pigs required less tending and smaller pastures.

This food arrangement, necessitated by the demands of King Tobacco, allowed for virtually no African influence in the cuisine of Maryland. Since the population was 60 to 70 percent white, the English cooking style prevailed with some passing nods to the Native Americans. Wheat and rye were grown starting in the 1730s, but slaves preferred corn and it provided better nutrition for the long days in the field. Most meals were one-pot affairs with the vegetables and whatever protein was available cooked together with water. Indeed, this style of cooking was one thing the English, African, and Native American cuisines all held in common.

These People Know How to Party

Of course, the early Maryland settlers were not completely unfamiliar with fine dining. As Frederick Philip Steiff wrote in his book *Eat, Drink, and be Merry in Maryland*, the English who settled here were "from the finest flower of Old England's Gentry." As such, they were accustomed to hosting lavish dinner parties with the finest delicacies. Their estates usually featured gardens and smokehouses. With no refrigeration, the curing of meats was critical and the residents along the Bay spiced their foods with mace, nutmeg, and cloves predominantly. The homes themselves were decked out with wine cellars, large pantries, and expansive dining rooms. Elaborate meals featured freshly caught terrapin, Chincoteague oysters, and myriad fish including blue, rock, sea trout, perch, and largemouth bass. To make sure the festivities remained merry, entire parties were built around sampling Madeira brought to America along the new trade routes.

One such member of this elite class was Augustine Herrman (c.1621-1686), who created the first map of Maryland in 1674. As payment for creating the map, Lord Baltimore gave him a thirty-one-and-a-half-square-mile piece of land between the Elk and Oppoquimimi Rivers eastward toward the Delaware line. In honor of his homeland, Herrman renamed the river Bohemia and called his estate Bohemia Manor. A tobacco plantation that also made indigo, a dye obtained from plants in the *indigofera* genus, Bohemia Manor became known for its culinary orgies of meat and drink. Herrman went so far as to create a private deer park on the property.

Even as the high life of colonial living was taking hold on the tobacco plantations, a cultural and economic shift was about to disrupt the prosperous world of the landed gentry. By the early 1700s, the odd mix of convicts, indentured servants, and black slaves working on the plantations created a roiling soup of discontent. The Native Americans, who had no understanding of whites owning blacks as property, mixed freely with the African transplants, adding fuel to an already building fire of white hostility toward the Indian tribes. While the Native Americans eventually moved to new territory, the convicts and indentured servants who in time won their freedom had few options. Some managed to find small plots of land to work, but most did not have the means to make a decent living at farming. An easier and more lucrative career could be made out of tonging oysters, fishing, or building boats. Instead of working the land along the Chesapeake, it was the Chesapeake Bay itself that became a source of income and subsistence.

The city of Annapolis on the western shore was a clear sign of the influence that the fishing trade was having on Maryland's changing economy. The first Baroque-style city in America, Annapolis was also known as the Ancient City. A fashionable society culture developed there, including the famous men-only Tuesday Club. Its members included painter Charles Willson Peale (1741-1827), who would later create several portraits of George Washington. In 1695, the new governor of Maryland, Francis Nicholson (1655-1728), moved the state capital to Annapolis from St. Mary's City. That first Maryland colony, so critical to the early development of the tobacco trade, was gone completely by 1720. A few years later in 1729, "Baltimore Town," north of Annapolis, was established as a port city and a center for shipbuilding.

Shipping, Canning, and the Iron Age

Emphasis on shipping and fishing created new opportunities for diversification. Areas along the Eastern Shore, which were never good for growing tobacco, suddenly became valuable for their natural resources. The abundance of pine and cypress trees in Talbot, Somerset, and Dorchester Counties provided not only raw lumber for shipbuilding but tar and turpentine as well. Oak, the most prominent species of tree in Maryland, was necessary for the skeleton and skin of most ships during the 1700s. Iron ore and hemp could also be found along the Bay's rivers and sheltered coves.

The shift away from tobacco also brought about a diversification in the economy that colonists welcomed. Unlike the predominantly male hordes of fortune seekers who flocked to the New World for instant riches, the eighteenth-century colonists had families and a desire for a more civilized life. Smaller industries like textiles and brewing took hold, and Smith Island added flax farming to its fishing interests. By 1767, hemp exports were giving tobacco a run for its money.

Ships were still most important, however, and the Western Shore began to dominate the economy. The Baltimore Clipper ships were world-class speed vessels and, as the Revolutionary War brewed, the ability to move goods and personnel quickly grew increasingly important. The first Navy ships were launched from the Harris Creek shipyard in Fells Point. The Eastern Shore, which had once benefited from providing the raw materials for shipbuilding, began to see this avenue of income dry up as shipbuilders switched to using iron for much of the ship's construction. The almost disastrous deforestation that was occurring on the Eastern Shore would have brought this revenue stream to an end anyway. By the close of the 1700s, Maryland was the national leader in shipbuilding and Baltimore was the clear leader in the Chesapeake Bay.

The death of King Tobacco and the rise of fishing and shipping created new opportunities for African-Americans as well. Slave owning became an economic liability for some and a moral dilemma for others like the Methodist Church. As early as 1745, over sixty free blacks were living in Somerset County as farmers and property owners. Black slaves were used increasingly as seamen, where the need for close teamwork allowed for greater freedom and responsibility. By 1796, the federal government issued Seamen's Protection Certificates for black merchant mariners, declaring them "citizens." While blacks were still forbidden from captaining registered vessels, many newly freed blacks found gainful employment by tonging for the plentiful and quite-in-demand oysters. By the time Frederick Douglass made his daring flight to freedom disguised as a free seaman, the United States was employing about one hundred thousand seamen per year, one-fifth of whom were black.

The development of new canning processes allowed for the distribution of canned oysters to all parts of the growing country. With its large port and railway access, Baltimore added oyster canning to its wealth of industries. Over one hundred packing houses populated the city, providing jobs for the flocks of European immigrants arriving in the United States for a new life.

The iron industry also created new jobs. As iron ships replaced wooden ones, iron production grew. At least fifteen foundries were operational in Baltimore by the end of the Revolutionary War. A century later, major iron producers like Columbia Iron Works and the Pennsylvania Steel Company (later known as Bethlehem Steel) dominated the commerce of Baltimore.

With people from Ireland, Germany, Russia, Poland, and other countries reaching Maryland's shores, one might think that the long-standing English influence on local cuisine would change. However, except for the introduction of some elements like sauerkraut (which some Marylanders, German or not, continue to incorporate into their Thanksgiving meals), Maryland dishes remained relatively straightforward and, of course, seafood was always prominent. The famous Baltimore writer and iconoclast H.L. Mencken (1880-1956), himself of German descent, wrote at length about Baltimore cuisine. A typical lunch from his childhood would include a platter of Norfolk spots, Himalaya corn cakes, succotash, buttered beets, baked potatoes, and string beans. If they were in season, oranges and bananas were eaten for dessert.

Mencken lived the vast majority of his life at 1524 Hollins Street, a three-story row house in the West Baltimore neighborhood known as Union Square. Some of his earliest memories are of his mother going to the fishmongers on Hollins Street to buy eight-inch blue crabs "with snow white meat almost as firm as soap" for ten cents per dozen. The rarer soft crabs were more expensive at 2½ cents each. When his mother reported to his father that the price of a twenty-inch shad had gone from 40 cents to 50 cents, his father predicted that the Republic would not survive the nineteenth century.

To Mencken, the popular Maryland oyster was low-class food eaten by drunks in oyster houses like Kelly's on Eutaw Street. He preferred blue crabs, particularly in crab soup. Mencken remembered how a former sheriff of Baltimore, Tom McNulty, had a special way of preparing soft shell crabs. He would spear a slice of bacon on a large fork, jam a soft shelled crab on top, and hold the fork over a charcoal brazier until the fat melted over the crab. Then he would slap it on a slice of hot toast.

East Meets West

While the Western Shore grew in population and commerce, the Eastern Shore became virtually frozen in time, bordered on one side by the Chesapeake Bay and on the other by the Atlantic Ocean. Fishing and farming remained its primary industries, allowing the land to recover from the ecological devastation it faced during the previous century. Its relatively small population and remoteness became part of the Eastern Shore's charm. Places like Smith Island, where everything must be brought in by boat, developed its own unique culture and dialect. Smith Island is best known today for its multi-layered eponymous cake, Maryland's official state dessert.

Soon, people on the Western Shore who were tired of the congestion and pollution that industrialization brought were taking vacations to the more pastoral land on the other side of the Bay. Just getting to the Eastern Shore, however, was a bit of an adventure. Vacationers would often spend an entire day on trains and ferries just to visit one of the small resort towns. For those seeking some surf and sun on the Atlantic side, the trip was even more complicated.

That all changed in 1952 when the first span of the William Preston Lane, Jr. Memorial Bridge (commonly known as the Bay Bridge) was built across the Chesapeake Bay. Covering over four miles, the massive bridge allowed travelers the ability to traverse in minutes what would once have taken hours. The bridge proved so popular, a second span was built in 1973.

© Jay Fleming

Even with two bridges connecting the Western Shore with the Eastern Shore, the traffic congestion over the twin spans is often quite heavy, especially in the summer months.

What a Fine Mess!

The mighty industrial surge to create the weapons of battle during World War II lured people from the south to Maryland where blue-collar jobs were plentiful. Even after the end of the conflict, businesses like Martin-Marietta, Bethlehem Steel, and General Motors fueled the population growth of Maryland. By the middle of the twentieth century, industrial runoff and overfishing placed terrible stresses on the Bay's ecosystem. However, it wasn't until the 1960s that scientists from area universities began to study the problem seriously. For example, because mollusks can concentrate chemical materials within their tissues, large quantities of heavy metals were detected in the oyster population. Also, the diversity of species was

declining. By the early 1970s, research expanded to other commercially viable species like soft- and hard-shell clams. Dredging to accommodate larger ships, sewage pollution due to inadequate treatment plants, the protection of wetlands from developers, and industrial pollution were heavy on the minds of scientists and conservationists during this time, but while there was a great deal of research going on, little or no effort was being made to implement a plan to save the Bay.

Then the National Science Foundation (NSF) outlined a plan to stimulate research efforts that focused on the needs of society with coordinated, problem-oriented research. Scientists from Johns Hopkins, the University of Maryland, and the Virginia Institute of Marine Sciences made proposals to a thirteen-member panel, which then coordinated with research institutions and agencies. Meanwhile, the Maryland Department of Natural Resources was established to coordinate efforts with local and federal agencies. The new spate of research and analysis prompted legislators to pass fifteen environmental laws in 1970 alone.

Efforts to clean up the Bay and research its flora and fauna continued through the 1970s. In 1977, federal and state programs came together to formulate a pragmatic plan that would renew deteriorating habitats. The Chesapeake Bay Agreement of 1983 was signed by Maryland and the surrounding states. Additional efforts were put into place in 1987 and the Chesapeake 2000 project took steps to improve water quality and protect living resources.

Still, with such a concentrated effort to restore the ecological health of the Bay, the struggle continues to find a balance between maintaining the fragile demands of the Bay's ecosystem and the needs of Marylanders, who are addicted to crabs, oysters, and rockfish as well as the sweet white corn and chickens raised on its shores. These staples of our diet, and the lifestyle surrounding the procurement of these staples, provide an identity for Marylanders far more evident than any ethnic heritage. The Bay sustains us, so we must sustain the Bay.

Part 2
Maryland's Protein Factory

There's no doubt about it—the first things that come to the minds of many Marylanders, when they hear the words "Chesapeake Bay," are crabs, crab cakes, and Old Bay® Seasoning. Maybe rockfish. For lots of folks, the Chesapeake happens to be: 1) the place that crabs come from; 2) the body of water that separates us from our favorite vacation spot, Ocean City, Maryland. But that's mostly the land-lubbing city dwellers on the west side of Maryland, the folks from Baltimore, Bel Air, Columbia, Glen Burnie, Silver Spring, etc. The people who live on the Bay, on either the western or Eastern Shore, or near one of the tributary rivers, know that the Chesapeake provides far more to Marylanders than just crabs and rockfish. For while the savory blue crab may be the best-known denizen of the deep, there are also three hundred or so species of fish living in the Chesapeake, many of which are eminently edible and have sustained the state's population since colonial times. And then there are the lowly bottom-dwelling oysters, perhaps the most important creatures to have lived in the waters of the Chesapeake Bay.

Never Mind the Mollusks: Here's the Chesapeake Oysters

Among the most popular creatures found in the Chesapeake Bay are *Crassostrea virginica*, otherwise known as the eastern oyster. Once upon a time, there were lots and lots of these tasty mollusks in the waters around the colonies, as evidenced by the ancient middens, or piles of discarded oyster shells, found along the coastline. Going back millennia, the oyster was a regular part of a Native American's diet. Archeologists have found layers of oyster shells thousands of years old along the shores of the Chesapeake. At Pope's Creek, a known ancient Native American settlement, a spread of oyster shells spanning 30 acres was found. Little wonder the Algonquins called

© Jay Fleming

the vast body of water that cut through their lands *Chesepiooc*, meaning "great shellfish bay." When the Europeans arrived, they soon learned from the Native Americans how delicious oysters were and ate their fill (and perhaps more).

At first, the oysters were harvested by hand or by tonging. Since oysters tend to spawn in clusters along the water bottom, early watermen using sailboats known as log canoes would drag a rock or chain attached to a rope along the sea bed. Once they could feel the rock or chain tapping on shells, they would lay anchor and proceed to pull up the oysters. Oyster tongs are scissors-like devices with long handles thirty-five feet or more in length. At the end of the handles are iron baskets with teeth to scoop up the oysters and bring them to the surface. The waterman must repeatedly scissor the handles until the teeth close together and form a tight trap around what could be as much as a third of a bushel of oysters. This taxing labor earned oyster tongs the nickname of "widow sticks."

Oysters became a valuable commodity, however, and many men chose this punishing way of life over the equally demanding but less certain occupation of farming. In the 1800s, watermen adopted a new method to gather the valuable mollusks in larger numbers. Dredging involves a contraption with metal teeth that is dragged along the bottom of a body of water, dislodging shellfish that are then gathered in a large mesh net. This is (sorta, almost) fine for deeper waters, but eventually dredgers worked the shallow waters in the same manner, damaging oyster reefs in the process. Dredging also creates soil displacement, which changes the salinity of the water and can eliminate or dislocate desirable species. While dredging was just dandy for the watermen at first, it soon became a catalyst to catastrophe.

The World's Oyster

Not only a Chesapeake Bay delicacy, oysters were also harvested and consumed in vast quantities in New York and New England. So much so that the ancient beds in New York and Boston harbors, which had in the past supplied generations of Native Americans with luscious bivalves, were soon depleted, or close to it. Back in those days, the Chesapeake still had a good number of *C. virginica* and crafty Yankees got the idea that they'd just float down and take them. So they brought their dredges and *took our oysters*. Just ripped them out of the Bay to send back home. As you might imagine, that didn't go down very well. Oyster fishing was a lucrative business, and there were plenty of oystermen in Maryland who didn't want to share with the folks from up north. They didn't really want to share with other oystermen, either, especially not the ones from Virginia, who felt they had a fair claim, since the Chesapeake stretches down into their state for a considerable distance as well.

In the nineteenth century, the Chesapeake had become the source for about half of the world's oyster supply. Not only was it feeding the locals, but the dawn of the Industrial Revolution meant that new technologies allowed for Chesapeake oysters to be sent around the globe. Commercial canning, a huge advancement in food preservation, became big business; oyster canneries dotted the coastline of both Maryland and Virginia. The work was hard, and freed slaves and white men worked side by side to process the millions of oysters needed to meet worldwide demand. So when watermen from New York to Connecticut came down for their piece of the action, it was not appreciated. The first oyster-related laws started to hit the books by 1820, when Maryland banned dredging. In 1830, the Maryland General Assembly passed legislation that allowed only Maryland residents to harvest oysters from Maryland waters. Then, in 1865, the state passed another law saying that harvesting required an annual permit. The oyster pirates weren't deterred by anything so minor as a law, so in 1868, Maryland created the Oyster Navy to fight what had by that time become a war. It patrolled the waters of the Chesapeake looking for illegal dredging activity being carried on by both local watermen and interlopers from other states.

The oyster wars were waged into the 1960s, when Maryland relented and allowed dredging in the Potomac. Despite efforts such as residence and licensing requirements for dredgers and private fishing rights in tributaries, the problem of over-harvesting had merely been delayed. Oyster populations dropped steadily during the twentieth century, from eight to ten million bushels per year in the early 1900s to just two to three million bushels by 1971. But oyster poaching and over-harvesting weren't the only problems. Two diseases—MSX and Dermo—hit the Chesapeake oyster population hard. The latter was discovered in the late 1940s, and the former ten years later. Fortunately, neither disease affects humans, but they certainly did a number on *C. virginica*.

A few years back, state and federal officials were toying with the idea of transplanting a species of Asian oyster in the Bay. As some scientists believe MSX entered the Chesapeake via Japanese oysters intentionally introduced to the Delaware Bay, this didn't seem like a particularly good idea. Thankfully, this idea was dumped. And it seems that wild oysters that are exposed to both diseases have started to exhibit signs of resistance.

An Oyster by Any Other Name

Now that we've gotten way ahead of ourselves, we should probably answer the question: So what exactly is an oyster?

For our purposes, an oyster is a bivalve mollusk, specifically *Crassostrea virginica*. That little beige blob in the oyster shell is a living, breathing (well, not breathing exactly) animal with thoughts and feelings just like ours (a lie). It is an animal, however, one with a somewhat complex lifecycle for something we think of as an appetizer. They start out as eggs, then become trochophores, veligers, pediveligers (all three are stages of larvae, and yes, pediveligers do have a foot), and spat, before becoming what we know as an oyster. At the spat stage, they start to resemble adult oysters, though teeny

© Kathy Wielech Patterson

tiny versions of them. It doesn't take all that long for spat to grow, however, doubling in size every two or three days.

At the point of sexual maturity, finding a mate is all about chemistry. Literally. Unlike crab mating, which we'll get into later, sexytime for oysters is anything but romantic. For much of the year, an oyster stores up glycogen, a form of glucose, which makes it fat and tasty. Then, when the water is warm enough (around 70°F), the oyster chooses a sex and diverts its energy to its sex organs. Eastern oysters are simultaneous hermaphrodites, meaning they have both male and female sexual organs. During the first months

© Jay Fleming

of life, most oysters are male. Then some of them change to female when they reach maturity. Others spawn a couple of times as males before becoming female, and still others, once female, go back to being male. When the oyster is ready to spawn, it will secrete pheromones, telling all the other oysters that it's orgy time (well, as much of an orgy that organisms that won't even touch can have). And then it releases eggs or sperm into the water column, depending on its sex at the moment. Hopefully all those eggs and sperm will bump into each other and fertilize. Even if they do, the odds are against them: only about 1 percent of fertilized eggs become larvae.

All this changing sex and spawning stuff usually occurs in months that do not contain the letter R, which is why oysters are not typically on the dinner menu in the summer. At this time, their bodies are either mostly gonads, or their flesh is weak and watery after the strain of reproducing. However, there are oysters that are perfectly fine to eat year-round: triploids. They have three sets of chromosomes and practice abstinence. That is, they don't spawn. And they grow faster than oysters that do spawn. While they sound like a bit of a freak of nature, don't judge—bananas, seedless watermelon, and blueberries are also triploids.

Triploids are farmed oysters. And farmed oysters may be the future of the Bay.

Old MacDonald Had an Oyster Farm

Generally, aquaculture gets mixed reactions. While it might be a good way to raise large numbers of fish in a contained area that makes them easy to gather up and send to market, there are factors involved that make this system bad for both the creature being raised and the environment in which it grows. Farmed salmon is one example. Much like some of us, farmed salmon eat processed food and get little exercise. They're fattier, but while they may contain a bit more of the Omega-3s we're told we should consume, their fat also can hold on to contaminants that might be in the water in which they live. And because the fish are living within a confined space, there's lots of poop building up in one place, which, before the giant nets of fish moved in, had been habitat for other species.

None of that is true for oysters. Oysters are filter feeders, sucking in water at a rate of up to fifty gallons per day, removing the nutrients that they need, and spitting out water that was cleaner than before it went in. It's thought that when the oyster population was at its peak it was able to filter the Chesapeake's 18 trillion gallons in one week. Today, it would take the Bay's current population about a year. So having more oysters in the water doing what they do naturally is beneficial. And yes, oysters poop. However, wild or farmed, oysters are not mobile creatures. Once they cement themselves down to a reef, whether it's natural or man-made, they're there for quite a while. Oysters hang out in clumps anyway, filtering and pooping together, so raising them in cages doesn't damage the ecosystem any more than raising them on reefs. In fact, because the oysters are around and the water is cleaner, other filter feeding creatures, like sea squirts and barnacles, come around and pitch in to make the benthic (bottom-dwelling) community a healthier habitat.

When you think about it this way, being called a "bottom feeder" isn't necessarily a bad thing.

While they've been farming oysters in Virginia for a while now, Maryland's only been doing it for a handful of years. Still, there are currently hundreds of aquaculture leases on the books and more enterprising wanna-be oyster farmers are signing up every year. Some folks are growing diploid oysters that spawn, in the hopes that their babies will help beef up the wild oysters. Others are growing triploids for the commercial market. Though these oysters are not helping to rebuild the once teeming oyster population, they are still doing their thing to clean the Bay.

So where do triploids come from exactly? From a lab, of course. Dr. Standish K. Allen, Jr., of the Virginia Institute of Marine Science at William & Mary, developed the first triploid oysters while still a student in the 1970s. He perfected the process a decade later. In the original process, a chemical was used to interrupt meiosis, or cell division. The new process required tetraploid oysters, or oysters with four sets of chromosomes—two sets too many. When these tetraploids, which Allen developed with fellow mollusk geneticist Ximing Guo, are bred with diploid oysters that have the normal two sets of chromosomes (as we humans do), they create infertile oysters that end up with three sets. Basically, even sets = fertile, odd sets = infertile. Dr. Allen has also worked to develop disease-resistant oysters via selective breeding, which along with triploidy, are "leading the charge of oyster aquaculture." And we thank him for that.

Bring 'Em Back Alive

While commercial farming is one solution for keeping a continuous flow of oysters from the Bay to the dinner table (while cleaning the water as well), several groups are hard at work to rejuvenate the wild oyster population. Oyster depletion has been a hot button topic for several decades now. In the early 1990s, the oyster population dropped off so precipitously that then Maryland Governor William Donald Schaefer appointed a forty-person task force to figure out what happened to the oysters. Three major reasons were uncovered: loss of habitat, disease (MSX and Dermo), and overfishing. The group determined that Mother Nature could not restore oysters on its own, so they recommended that the state invest in a long-term oyster restoration project. The task force also recommended that the organization set up to do the work be a non-profit rather than another government agency. The non-profit group known as Chesapeake Appreciation, Inc. became the Oyster Recovery Partnership (ORP) in 1994 with these specific initiatives incorporated into their mission.

© Timothy Devine

The ORP coordinates with various agencies involved in repopulating the Bay with oysters. From the latter part of the twentieth century and into the early 2000s, government agencies focused a tremendous amount of time and money on trying to address the issue. Between 1994 and 2008, federal and state officials spent 39.7 million dollars in Maryland alone, with another nineteen million dollars spent in Virginia. Oyster habitat was built, but there were disputes over the proper height. Some officials insisted on reefs a foot or more high so the oysters would stay out of the mud, but the state built shorter reefs saying that the taller reefs were too expensive. The U.S. Army Corp of Engineers said otherwise and had success with taller reefs. Still, oyster numbers continued to decline during that same period, with one estimate stating the population was down by about 20 percent. One issue raised was that most of the oysters created by these preservation efforts were snatched up by watermen too quickly. The oysters that survived the pollution and disease, and were the best candidates to spawn other healthy oysters, were instead harvested right away.

© Jay Fleming

New reef construction has kept watermen from harvestable waters for periods of time, causing not a small bit of consternation. A huge, ongoing reef-building effort conducted by the Maryland Oyster Restoration Interagency Workgroup (comprising the U.S. Army Corps of Engineers, Maryland Department of Natural Resources, the National Oceanic and Atmospheric Administration, the ORP, and others), known as the Choptank River Complex Project, aims to restore 370 acres of oyster habitat in Harris Creek and the Little Choptank and Tred Avon rivers. The project faced delays due to the concerns of watermen over some of the building materials being used for the reef restoration, namely granite quarried in Havre de Grace and fossilized shell from Florida. It was felt that the heavy rock might affect trotlining crabbers, and the shell, some of which seemed to have some clay intermingled, might dirty the river. Valid concerns, but the project so far has been proceeding with legal permits from the proper agencies. And it has been an absolute success—the oyster population in the Choptank Complex Project area has been going gangbusters.

With more reefs restored and more oyster spat planted comes more habitat and more adult oysters, all of which equals bigger harvests. But this takes time. The Bay's current oyster population is still miniscule compared to historical numbers, but the oyster harvest has increased a bit in the past few years. However, there are also more licensed oystermen in the area, so the threat of overharvesting continues.

Pearls of Wisdom

We're going to debunk a long-standing myth for you right now. Pearls do not come from oysters. They actually come from a kind of saltwater clam from the genus *Pinctada*, family Pteriidae. Edible oysters, like *Crassostrea virginica*, the oysters found in the Chesapeake Bay, belong to the genus *Ostrea* and the family Ostreidae. They're not closely related at all.

If you pry open the shell of a pearl-producing mollusk, you'll find the inside coated with a lovely "pearlescent" (for lack of a better term) substance. This is the mother-of-pearl one finds in jewelry, antique inlaid furniture, etc. This same substance, when produced in layers over a round irritant (like a grain of sand), is known as "nacre." A pearl's value is dependent on the quality, translucency, and number of layers of nacre it has. The more layers of nacre, the more lustrous the pearl. Natural pearls, those created without the intervention of humans, are extremely rare and, thus, also very valuable. Most pearls are "cultured," that is, a small nucleus of polished mussel shell is inserted into the pearl-producing mollusk, which then secretes layers of nacre over it. When the pearl reaches the desired size, usually after a couple of years, it's removed. The same mollusk can be reseeded three or four times in its life, and some of them can bear multiple pearls at the same time.

© Kathy Wielech Patterson

That's not to say that one won't find a "pearl" in an edible oyster. You're probably even thinking, "Ha! I've found pearls in oysters before!" It is true that most mollusks have the ability to secrete a substance over an irritant that makes its way into the shell. But that substance doesn't have the lovely iridescent sheen of mother-of-pearl. It's probably just the same dull white of the interior of the oyster you found it in. That "pearl" is about as valuable as a kidney stone.

Another factoid to blow your mind: Many of the pearls on the market today aren't even made by "pearl oysters." If they're labeled "freshwater pearls," they come from mussels. And no, they're not the same mussels as the ones you had for dinner last night, steamed in white wine sauce with a side of *frites*.

Oysters, of course, are best when they're super fresh, cooked and consumed immediately after shucking. If you don't have easy access to in-shell oysters, then you can use the ones sold in pint containers at your local grocery store, just don't eat them raw.

Chesapeake Bay Oyster Shooter with Cucumber Fish Pepper Mignonette

COURTESY OF BRENDAN DORR, B & O AMERICAN BRASSERIE

This flavorful mouthful (or two) incorporates three of Maryland's own: oysters, fish peppers, and Sloop Betty Vodka. The vodka is a product of Blackwater Distilling just over the Bay Bridge in the Eastern Shore town of Stevensville, Maryland. Fish peppers are an attractively striped heirloom chile pepper that was once grown exclusively by African-Americans in the Chesapeake region. It has recently made a resurgence and has been spotted on the menu of Baltimore-area upscale restaurants.

(THE MIGNONETTE IS ENOUGH FOR TWENTY-FOUR OYSTERS)

For the mignonette:

½ cup rice wine vinegar

½ minced shallot

1 small piece ginger, grated

¼ peeled and chopped cucumber

½ fish pepper, finely chopped

1½ teaspoons sugar

1 pinch fresh ground black pepper

For each shooter:

1 shucked oyster on the half shell

1 ounce chilled Sloop Betty or other high-quality vodka

1 tablespoon cucumber fish pepper mignonette

To make the mignonette: Combine all ingredients in a small mixing bowl. Gently whisk to mix. Cover and refrigerate for at least 1 hour before use. Can be prepped a day before.

For each shooter: Spoon some mignonette onto the oyster. Pour the chilled vodka shot into a rocks glass. Slurp the oyster and drink the shot.

Basic Mignonette Sauce

Some people like their raw oysters plain, with nothing but their own liquor to flavor them. Others prefer a bit of acid, like a squeeze of lemon juice or this classic combination of wine vinegar and shallot.

(ENOUGH FOR ABOUT TWELVE OYSTERS)

¼ cup red wine vinegar

1 tablespoon finely chopped shallot

Salt and freshly ground pepper to taste

Combine ingredients and chill. Spoon over chilled oysters on the half shell.

Bloody Mary Mignonette

There are oyster farmers who shudder at the thought of their hard work being drowned in a sweet cocktail sauce full of horseradish, but that's the way some people eat 'em. This mignonette sauce might be a compromise. It has tomato and horseradish, like cocktail sauce, but it's still primarily a light, vinegar-based sauce that highlights rather than buries an oyster's fresh brininess.

(ENOUGH FOR ABOUT EIGHTEEN OYSTERS)

¼ cup red wine vinegar

2 tablespoons vodka

1 tablespoon tomato sauce

1 tablespoon finely minced shallot

1 teaspoon finely minced celery

1 teaspoon prepared horseradish

1 shake Worcestershire sauce

Pinch sugar

Dash hot sauce

Squeeze of lemon juice

Salt and freshly ground pepper to taste

Combine ingredients and chill. Spoon over chilled oysters on the half shell.

Shucking an Oyster

There is more than one way to shuck an oyster. There's the wrong way, of course, and then there's the correct way. If you're a professional oyster shucker, then you can just skip the rest of this section, but if you're a layman (or the former restaurant owner who we watched butcher a pile of poor defenseless bivalves a few years back), you might want to pay attention.

Besides a supply of fresh oysters, you'll need two important tools: an oyster knife and a tea towel. An oyster knife has a short blade without a cutting edge. The tip is flat and pointed, and while not as pointy as say, a steak knife, it can do some damage if you stab yourself in the hand with it. This is where the tea towel comes in.

Fold the towel in half lengthwise and put it down on a flat surface. Pick up an oyster and hold it so the rounded cup is facing downward. Find the hinge where the top and bottom shell meet (this should be on the end where the cup is deepest); this is where you will insert the knife. If you are right-handed, put the oyster down on the towel with the hinge end facing right (the opposite if you are left-handed). Fold the left side of the towel up over and covering the oyster, then fold the edge back onto the oyster so it's mostly covered but the hinge is still visible. This way, you have a double-thickness of towel separating your hand from the oyster, and thus the knife as well.

Hold the oyster down firmly with your non-dominant hand. With your dominant hand on the knife handle, insert the knife tip into the hinge and push it in about a quarter inch. You might need to re-insert it at slightly different angles, as the hinge will vary from mollusk to mollusk. Once you feel you have the knife tip well into the hinge, twist the knife to pop the shell open. If you twist before you have the tip in far enough, you risk chipping off a chunk of shell, so be patient. It takes a couple of tries to get the feel of things.

Place the oyster on the towel

The shell won't pop off all the way; the oyster is connected to both top and bottom. Gently run the blade of the knife in a smooth motion along the contour of the top shell, releasing the oyster. Pull off the top shell carefully, so as not to spill any of the liquor, and use the knife again to scrape the oyster from the bottom shell. Using a paper towel, gently wipe the inner edge of the oyster to remove any grit or shell pieces. Place the oyster on a bed of crushed ice on a plate until you're ready to eat it, or just slurp away.

Fold the towel over the oyster

Insert the knife into the hinge

Smoked Oysters with Old Bay® Seasoning Butter

COURTESY OF CHEF ZACK MILLS, WIT & WISDOM

Much like drawn butter on lobster, the zesty herbed butter brings out the best in the warm, smoky, oysters.
(MAKES 2–4 SERVINGS)

8 ounces unsalted butter, at room temperature

Zest and juice of 1 lemon

1 teaspoon finely chopped parsley

1 teaspoon finely chopped chives

1 teaspoon finely chopped tarragon

1 teaspoon Old Bay® Seasoning

12 oysters

Place butter, lemon zest and juice, herbs, and Old Bay® Seasoning into a stand mixer with a paddle attachment. Whip on medium speed until combined. Scrape into a plastic container with a lid and set aside until ready to use.

Shuck oysters and make sure they are released from the shell. Top each with a teaspoon of the seasoned butter. Place oysters on a hot grill or smoker. Close the lid and allow to cook until they are warmed through and just begin to curl.

Serve oysters on a bed of salt to keep them from tipping over and spilling the butter.

© Zack Mills

Pickled Oysters with Warm Chicory Salad and Sauce Romesco

COURTESY OF CHEF KEITH LONG, HARVEST WOOD GRILL + TAP

Back in the old days, before refrigeration, pickling was a fine way to preserve oysters. They were boiled in vinegar with generous amounts of spices like mace, allspice, and white pepper, then stored in a stoneware crock someplace cool and dark. Today, there's no need to pickle oysters for preservation purposes. We pickle them because . . . well, because they taste good, not unlike an oyster on the half shell doused with a good quantity of mignonette sauce. The vinegar should pique the palate, but let the oyster flavor shine through. It's best not to boil the oysters in the vinaigrette over heat, lest they get overcooked. In this recipe, the oysters are barely cooked in a super-flavorful liquid touched with the citrusy addition of herbal tea before being tossed with a salad of wilted bitter greens and a rich pepper sauce. (SERVES 4–6)

For pickling liquid and oysters:

1½ cups champagne vinegar

½ cup vinegar de Normandy, or apple cider vinegar

1 lemon verbena tea bag

1 juniper berry

1 allspice berry

4 fresh bay leaves

¼ cup kosher salt

½ cup light brown sugar

¼ teaspoon red chile flakes

½ teaspoon pink peppercorns

½ tablespoon yellow mustard seed

3 tablespoons extra virgin olive oil

1 tablespoon sea salt

For the sauce Romesco:

1 (12-ounce) can roasted pequillo peppers, drained

1 clove garlic

1 ounce smoked Marcona almonds

1 tablespoon grated Parmesan cheese

1½ tablespoons sherry vinegar

For salad:

1 pound slab bacon, cut into lardons

1 shallot, minced

2 cloves garlic, chopped

½ cup cider vinegar

1 teaspoon salt

½ teaspoon pepper

24 oysters, shucked

3 bunches chicory (also known as curly endive or frisée)

To make pickling liquid: Combine all ingredients plus four and a half cups of water in a large pot and bring to a boil. Lower heat and reduce to a simmer. Cook for 8 minutes, then turn off the heat.

Put the oysters in a non-reactive (glass or ceramic) bowl. Strain the pickling liquid, then pour one quart of it over the oysters. Keep cool in refrigerator until ready to serve. (Reserve the remaining pickling liquid for future use; it works well with rock shrimp, mussels, etc.)

To make sauce: Combine all ingredients except the olive oil and salt in a high speed blender and gradually increase the speed to high. Once on high and the peppers are becoming a purée, slowly drizzle in the olive oil until all is incorporated. Season with salt to taste. Store in refrigerator for up to five days.

Note: If you cannot find smoked Marcona almonds, toast them in the oven at 350°F for 15 to 18 minutes until golden brown.

To make salad: Cook bacon until crisp. Without straining the fat, turn down the heat to low and add the shallot and garlic. Cook together for one minute or until lightly caramelized. Whisk in vinegar to create a broken vinaigrette and season with the salt and pepper. Keep warm until ready to serve.

To serve: Combine the oysters and chicory in a large mixing bowl. Slowly pour the warm dressing over, which should wilt the chicory slightly. Pour a small pool of warm romesco onto the center of a plate, then place dressed salad with oysters on top of sauce. Serve immediately.

Flying Dog Brewery

Flying Dog Brewery started life in 1990 as a brewpub in Aspen, Colorado, a partnership between an astrophysicist and a rancher. They won their first Great American Beer Festival award in 1991 for their Doggie Style pale ale. After several successful years in Colorado, Flying Dog purchased the Frederick Brewing Company in Frederick, Maryland, and in 2008 moved all beer production to Maryland.

Perhaps best known for their IPAs, Flying Dog has put out a wide variety of interesting brews over the years, including an Earl Grey Black Wheat beer, a Lemongrass Rice Ale, and a Mint Chocolate Stout. They've also put out two very Maryland-centric beers, Dead Rise and Pearl Necklace.

Dead Rise is a summer ale flavored with Old Bay® Seasoning. A deadrise, in boating terms, is the angle of the bottom of the hull in a cross-section view. A deadrise is also a type of traditional fishing boat used in the Chesapeake Bay. These heavy-duty boats are made to accommodate the various equipment—oyster dredges, crab pots, nets, culling boards—that Chesapeake watermen typically need to work. Flying Dog's namesake is a workhorse as well, a Belgian-style pale ale that works with just about any steamed or fried seafood and is a refreshing quaff on its own. Available from Memorial Day to Labor Day, sales of Dead Rise benefit the Maryland Department of Natural Resources' True Blue program. This labeling and promotion initiative allows consumers to tell which Maryland restaurants and other food service establishments use genuine Maryland blue crab in their crab cakes, soup, and what-have-you.

Pearl Necklace is an oyster stout brewed with Rappahannock River Oysters. While not tasting of oysters, this medium-bodied brew has typical roasty stout flavors and a butter-toffee finish, but also a slight briny quality, which makes it a perfect match to oysters, particularly oyster stew. Proceeds from the sale of Pearl Necklace benefit the Oyster Recovery Partnership, which has been instrumental in restoring oysters and oyster habitat to the Chesapeake Bay.

Fried Oysters

Some folks too squeamish to eat raw oysters have no problem downing a plate full of the mollusks if they're fried. Perhaps it's because their texture is a bit firmer once oyster meets oil, or maybe it's because pretty much everything tastes great after being coated in crumbs and given a bath in hot fat.

(SERVES 4)

1 cup all-purpose flour

Salt and freshly ground pepper

1 cup dry bread crumbs

2 eggs

2 tablespoons milk

1 stick unsalted butter

1 cup vegetable oil

1 pint shucked oysters, patted dry

Place the flour on a plate and season with salt and pepper. On another plate, place the bread crumbs; season with salt and pepper. Beat the eggs with the milk in a bowl.

Roll the oysters in the flour. Pat off excess, then dip them in the egg. Roll egg-coated oysters in the bread crumbs.

© Thinkstock

In a large, deep skillet or heavy saucepan, melt the butter and add the oil. Heat until sizzling.

Fry oysters in butter and oil mixture until golden brown on both sides, 2 to 3 minutes. Remove cooked oysters to paper towel–lined plates to drain. Season with additional salt and pepper and serve with tartar or cocktail sauce.

Tartar Sauce

Tartar sauce is a go-to accompaniment for crab cakes as well as fried oysters.
(MAKES ABOUT ¾ CUP)

½ cup mayonnaise

2 tablespoons lemon juice

1 tablespoon finely chopped cornichons

1 tablespoon capers

1 tablespoon grated onion

2 teaspoons finely chopped fresh parsley

½ teaspoon finely grated lemon zest

½ teaspoon Dijon mustard

½ teaspoon dried tarragon

4 shakes Worcestershire sauce

Combine all ingredients in a bowl. Refrigerate until ready to serve.

Cocktail Sauce

The large amount of horseradish in this zesty cocktail sauce makes it nice and spicy. If you prefer a milder sauce, reduce the horseradish accordingly. While, personally, we wouldn't think of putting this on anything other than steamed shrimp, many folks appreciate its tomato-y sweetness on both raw and cooked oysters.
(MAKES 1 CUP)

1 cup ketchup

1 tablespoon prepared horseradish

1 teaspoon fresh lemon juice

1 teaspoon Worcestershire sauce

Combine all ingredients in a bowl. Refrigerate until ready to serve.

Oyster Recovery Partnership

The Oyster Recovery Partnership (ORP) is a non-profit organization whose mission is to "plan, promote, and implement science-based and sustainable shellfish restoration, aquaculture, and wild fishery activities to protect our environment, support our economy, and preserve our cultural heritage." They work closely with other groups, including the Chesapeake Bay Foundation, the Maryland Department of Natural Resources, U.S. Army Corps of Engineers, National Oceanic and Atmospheric Administration, Maryland Watermen's Association, the University of Maryland Center for Environmental Science Horn Point Laboratory, and the Nature Conservancy, that have a common interest in Chesapeake Bay conservation.

The ORP started out life in 1972 as Chesapeake Appreciation, Inc. (CA). In 1993, a roundtable of Maryland businesses, institutions, and individuals formulated a plan for promoting oyster recovery. They determined that CA should be expanded in order to be better able to coordinate the efforts of a diverse group of partners who would put large-scale restoration programs into action. These programs would involve three major components: planting oysters, collecting shells to create oyster reefs; and promoting aquaculture. All three, of course, have one main goal: to increase the Bay's oyster population. The ORP has been successful. So far, they've planted more than five billion oysters on 1,600 acres of reef and repurposed tens of thousands of bushels of empty shells as new oyster habitat.

As of this writing, the ORP is working on the East Coast's biggest oyster restoration project ever, the Choptank River Complex Project. The Choptank is the largest river on the Delmarva Peninsula, and the goal is to restore and repopulate the river's oyster reefs. The hope is to use this project as a blueprint for other large-scale restoration projects throughout the Chesapeake and its tributaries.

The Shell Recycling Alliance (SRA) is the arm of the ORP responsible for shell collection. Seafood wholesalers and restaurants are encouraged to recycle their shells, as are consumers who are also encouraged to support SRA member restaurants and to save and donate any shells from oysters consumed at home. The State of Maryland offers a five-dollar-per-bushel tax credit for recycling oyster shells as an incentive to restaurants (and anyone else) to repurpose them rather than dump them in landfills. Once picked up from any of several locations throughout the state of Maryland, the shells are delivered to a central location where they are sun bleached for a year, then cleaned in giant washing machines. While the bulk of the shell used in reef restoration is purchased by the state from an oyster processing plant in Virginia, there still is not enough for the amount of restoration needed. So save those shells!

As for fostering aquaculture, there are several initiatives. One of the ORP's partners, the Ratcliffe Foundation, has been training watermen in the art of growing their own oysters. Fifty or so have completed the program thus far and have been encouraged to buy leases at the affordable price of $3.50 per underwater acre. Marylanders Grow Oysters has allowed homeowners to do just that—grow oysters—although not for personal consumption. Wire cages with hundreds of oysters are installed under private or community piers; after a year, the oysters within them are replanted on oyster sanctuaries to supplement the wild oyster population. And of course there are several successful commercial aquaculture ventures in the state of Maryland right now. Though many of them choose to grow triploid oysters, which do not spawn, they are as effective as "wild" oysters in filtering the waters of the Chesapeake.

Fried Oyster Banh Mi

Most people know about oyster po' boys, a famous submarine-style sandwich from Louisiana. They are delicious, but why not switch things up a bit and try a Vietnamese-style oyster sandwich with sweet and tangy pickled vegetables, a spicy mayo, and a good dose of cilantro. If you don't like cilantro, you can leave it off, of course, but it really makes the sandwich. (SERVES 4)

1 medium carrot, peeled

6 large red radishes

½ teaspoon salt

¼ cup sugar

½ cup rice vinegar

½ cup mayonnaise

1 tablespoon Vietnamese fish sauce

Sriracha hot sauce

1 tablespoon chopped scallion

4 (6-inch) pieces of baguette

1 recipe fried oysters (page xxx) using panko instead of regular bread crumbs

1 cucumber, peeled, seeded, and cut into about 3-inch strips

Cilantro

Cut the carrot and radishes into matchsticks.

Combine the salt, sugar, and vinegar in a bowl. Add half a cup of water and stir the mixture to dissolve the sugar. Marinate the vegetables in the brine for about an hour.

Combine the mayonnaise, fish sauce, and about 1 teaspoon of the sriracha. If you like spicy, add more to taste. Stir in the scallion and refrigerate until ready to use.

Halve baguettes lengthwise. If they seem doughy, pull out some of the insides and discard. Spread the bread with a bit of the mayonnaise and top with one-quarter of the oysters. Distribute the pickled vegetables and cucumber evenly over the oysters, and top with a generous amount of cilantro. Enjoy right away.

© Kathy Wielech Patterson

Classic Oyster Stew

Simplicity itself.
(SERVES 2–3)

1 pint shucked oysters with their liquor

4 tablespoons unsalted butter

2½ cups milk

½ cup heavy cream

Salt and pepper to taste

Chopped parsley and oyster crackers, for garnish

Drain the oysters and reserve the liquor. Melt the butter in a saucepan, add the oysters and cook just until they start to curl on the edges.

While the oysters are cooking, heat the milk and cream to a simmer with the reserved oyster liquor. Stir in the oysters with the butter from the pan. Season with salt and pepper to taste.

Serve with a sprinkle of parsley and a handful of oyster crackers.

© Thinkstock

Fried Oyster Stew

COURTESY OF CHEF SCOTT HINES, B&O AMERICAN BRASSERIE

This dish brings together the best of both worlds—a creamy, savory soup, with the crunch of fried oysters. And this stew is full of oyster flavor since there are pureed oysters in the broth in addition to the fried garnish.

(MAKES 12 SERVINGS)

For the oysters:

1 cup shaken buttermilk

Hot sauce, to taste

1 pint oysters

½ cup cornmeal

½ cup all-purpose flour

½ cup panko bread crumbs

1 tablespoon Old Bay® Seasoning

Oil for frying

For the stew:

½ pound bacon, cut into lardons

½ onion, cut into tiny dice

1 rib celery, cut into tiny dice

1 cup celery root, cut into tiny dice

1 shallot, minced

1 leek, washed thoroughly and cut into very thin slices

3 salt-packed anchovy fillets, chopped

White wine

1½ quarts chicken stock

1½ quarts heavy cream

1 Yukon gold potato, cut into small dice

Several sprigs fresh thyme

2 bay leaves

Freshly ground black pepper and kosher salt

1 pint oysters and their liquor

To make oysters: Place buttermilk in a bowl. Season with hot sauce. Add the oysters, reserving the liquor for the stew base. Let soak for about twenty minutes.

Whiz the cornmeal, flour, panko, and seasoning in a food processor. Pour into a large shallow bowl.

Heat about ½ inch of oil in a large heavy frying pan or cast iron skillet.

Take the oysters, shaking off excess buttermilk, and dredge them in the crumbs. Fry until brown on both sides, 2 to 3 minutes. Drain on paper towel–lined plates.

To make stew: Cook the bacon lardons in a large pot until they have rendered their fat and are crisp. Remove bacon to a bowl. Keep about 2 tablespoons of the bacon fat in the pot and discard the rest.

Cook vegetables and anchovy in bacon fat until just soft. Deglaze pan with a few glugs of white wine, scraping up any bits that have become stuck to the bottom. Stir in the cooked bacon, stock, cream, and potato. Tie the thyme and bay leaves together with a bit of kitchen twine and drop into the pot. Bring mixture to a boil, then turn off the heat to allow the potato to gently cook in the hot liquid. Season soup with plenty of black pepper and kosher salt to taste. Check for potato doneness after fifteen minutes; turn the heat back on for a few minutes if potato is still hard.

Remove one-third of the soup to a blender. Add the oysters and their liquor plus the reserved liquor from the fried oysters and blend to a puree. The soup will be hot at this point so make sure not to fill the blender all the way. Remove the plastic cap from the blender lid and cover with a kitchen towel. Hold towel down firmly while blending so hot soup won't slosh out. Pour pureed mixture back into soup pot. Cover pot and keep warm.

To serve: Ladle soup into bowls. Garnish with two or three fried oysters.

© Thinksto

Oyster and Bacon Pie

COURTESY OF CHEF ADAM SNYDER, BREW HOUSE NO. 16

How do you make oyster stew even better? Put a pie crust around it! This recipe calls for three cups of oyster liquor, which you might have on hand if you've shucked a lot of oysters for multiple recipes. If not, you can use bottled clam juice or fish stock. (SERVES 6–8)

For crust:

2½ cups all-purpose flour

1 teaspoon salt

1 teaspoon sugar

8 ounces cold unsalted butter, cut into ½-inch cubes

For filling:

½ pound slab bacon, cut into medium dice

2 ounces unsalted butter

2 cups diced celery

2 cups diced parsnips

2 cups diced yellow onion

¾ cup all-purpose flour

⅓ cup white wine

3 cups oyster liquor

4 cups diced potatoes

2 tablespoons whole grain mustard

1 cup heavy cream

1 pint shucked oysters

2 tablespoons minced parsley

Salt and pepper to taste

To assemble pie:

1 egg

To make crust: Combine flour, salt, and sugar in a food processor. Add butter and pulse until mixture resembles coarse meal, about 10 seconds.

With machine running, slowly add ¼ to ½ cup cold water until dough comes together and forms a ball. Turn the dough out onto a work surface and flatten it into a disk. Wrap in plastic and refrigerate at least an hour before using.

To make filling: In a large pot over medium heat render bacon in butter until crispy. Add celery, parsnips, and onions and cook until vegetables soften and sweat, about 8 minutes. Sprinkle in the flour and stir well to create a roux. Cook for 5 minutes. Pour in the wine and stir, scraping up any bits of vegetable clinging to the pan.

Add the oyster liquor and potatoes. Cook until liquid thickens, then stir in the mustard and heavy cream. Add the oysters, turn the heat to low, and cook for 20 minutes. Stir in parsley, add salt and pepper. Remove mixture from the heat, and allow to cool.

To assemble pie: Preheat oven to 325°F.

Scoop pie filling into a 4-quart oven-safe dish or casserole.

Roll pastry out to ⅛ inch thickness and drape over pie filling. Crimp edges decoratively. Beat egg with two tablespoons of water and brush it over the crust. Cut three slits into the top to allow steam to vent.

Bake for 30 minutes, until pastry is golden brown and filling is hot. Allow to rest 5 minutes before serving.

The Future of Chesapeake Products— Tim Devine of Barren Island Oysters

By his own admission, Tim Devine is a "hippie environmentalist," but before that, he was a professional photographer living and working in New York City. Once he got tired of the high-paced and superficial lifestyle of the big city, the Easton native decided to move back to Maryland and become an oyster farmer.

Barren Island Oysters is one of the few successful oyster farms currently operating in the state of Maryland, and, so far, the only one growing oysters in the actual Chesapeake Bay. His farm's "merroir" (the traits peculiar to its location) includes saltier waters and whatever flavors are coming off the eternally eroding Barren Island. When you factor in the runoff-protection provided by nearby Blackwater National Wildlife Refuge and the techniques Devine employs to grow them and get them ready for market, the final result is a unique oyster.

"I had to learn everything through trial and error," says Devine. "Nobody likes to share how they do things. Nobody would tell me anything." Everyone, however, was willing to tell him how he was going to fail.

Devine started off by asking chefs what they wanted in an oyster. Then he scouted locations by taking water samples. Barren Island wasn't terribly far from Washington D.C., which Devine perceived as his primary market, and it was far enough into the Bay to produce an oyster that had a noticeable bit of salt. (Other Maryland oysters are raised in rivers, where the salinity is neutral or non-existent.) Once he got his lease and permits, he invested in half a million oysters, built an upweller (like a baby oyster incubator of sorts), and planted his oysters himself from a tiny boat. More than half didn't survive. Devine was told he'd never sell the remaining oysters at the price he wanted, yet his first successful harvest sold out in six months.

In the four years since he started farming, Devine has learned a few things about oysters, but there's always more. "I have a good handle on knowing what I don't know. I'm getting better each year. It takes about ten years to hone anything." Among the things he's learned is that a lot of the equipment available to novice oyster farmers is meant for use in the waters of New England, not in the sediment-rich Chesapeake Bay. Unfortunately, it takes months for the results of using incorrect equipment to come to light, so Devine is constantly dreaming up new ways to better his process. "I'm always trying to figure things out. Making subtle changes." That includes the angle at which water flows into his upwellers, special cage designs, and even the amount of time his oysters rest between being tumbled and going to market. Devine recently teamed up with one of the best fabricators on the Eastern Shore to design a line of custom aquaculture equipment under the name Oysterworx and plans to sell his innovations to other newbie oyster farmers. Rather than having to learn through trial and error, they can "do things right" the first time, which is beneficial for everyone, from the farmer to the consumer.

Not everyone understands Devine's need to innovate. "Tim thinks too much," says one of his employees, a young local waterman. "He thinks about stuff that don't need thinking about." Judging by his success, we believe Tim Devine does exactly the right amount of thinking.

© Timothy Devine

Corn Bread and Oyster Dressing

What could be a more Maryland-style accompaniment to Thanksgiving dinner than a dressing that combines both corn and oysters?

(SERVES 6)

For corn bread:

2½ cups coarse yellow or white cornmeal

1½ teaspoons baking powder

1 teaspoon kosher salt

2 ounces unsalted butter, plus more for the pan

1½ cups milk

1 large egg, lightly beaten

For dressing:

6 ounces unsalted butter (1½ sticks) (divided use)

6 cups corn bread, cut into ½-inch cubes

1 medium onion, chopped

2 ribs celery, chopped

2 cloves garlic, crushed

4-5 fresh sage leaves, chopped

2 teaspoons fresh thyme

1 teaspoon kosher salt

¼ teaspoon cayenne pepper

Freshly ground black pepper to taste

1 dozen freshly shucked oysters and their liquor

1½ cups chicken broth, warmed

To make corn bread: Preheat oven to 425°F. Combine the cornmeal, baking powder, and salt in a large bowl. Melt butter in the microwave and combine with the milk. Whisk in the egg, then pour the wet ingredients into the cornmeal mixture. Whisk until smooth.

Generously grease a square 8- or 9-inch baking pan with butter. Pour in the batter and bake until corn bread is golden brown and a toothpick inserted in the center comes out clean, 20 to 25 minutes.

To make stuffing: Preheat oven to 400°F.

Melt one stick of the butter and toss with the corn bread. Spread on a baking sheet and bake until browned and lightly crisp on the outsides, about 20 minutes. Allow corn bread to cool on the baking sheet then transfer to a large bowl. Turn down the oven temperature to 350°F.

Melt the remaining half stick of butter in a large skillet over medium heat. Add the onion and celery and cook, stirring occasionally, until onions are translucent, about 5 minutes. Stir in the garlic and cook an additional minute or two. Add the cooked veg to the corn bread in the bowl plus the sage, thyme, salt and pepper, and toss. Chop the oysters and add them and their juices to the corn bread mixture. Drizzle the stock over the corn bread, using enough to moisten everything, but not make it soggy.

Pack the stuffing into a greased 10-inch cast iron skillet. Cover pan with foil and bake for 15 minutes, then remove foil and bake an additional 15 to 20 minutes, until top is golden brown. Serve hot.

Blue Is the Color of Our Crab

There's no one symbol that defines the State of Maryland more than the blue crab. Sure we have a state flag and a state flower and even a state dessert (more on that later), but if you travel around Maryland, you are likely to see far more images of the bi-clawed crustacean than any of these other symbols combined. Restaurant signs, government publicity literature, festival signs, and even the logos for local plumbers will find some way to work in a caricature of the crab. And most of these images will even show the crab as bright red, which is how most Marylanders see them after they've been steamed and dumped on a butcher paper–covered table set

Jay Fleming

with mallets. Marylanders are crazy about blue crabs, associating them not only with good eating, but also countless memorable summertime feasts with friends and family and pitchers of cold beer to soothe the burn of Old Bay® Seasoning.

For a long time, no one was really sure how far back the love of eating crabs went. While a large body of physical evidence has shown that both Native Americans and English colonists ate a significant amount of oysters, it was not as clear whether blue crabs were eaten in the same quantities. However, recent evidence indicates that these early residents ate far more crabs than originally thought. A comprehensive review of ninety-three archaeological sites across the Chesapeake Bay, dating back to 1,200 B.C., reveals that the blue crab was in fact a favorite even then. Everyone ate them. Crab remains were discovered at a Native American settlement dating from the 1600s, George Washington's Mount Vernon Estate, and plantations and manors across Maryland. It was also discovered that larger crabs were more common in prehistoric times than they are today. Not only does it appear that crabs were popular for millennia, but also that the modern smaller crabs of today are in part the result of intensive fishing that removed large crabs from the population.

According to Torben Rick, an anthropologist at the Smithsonian's National Museum of Natural History, and lead author of the study mentioned above, "Blue crabs were an important source of food for Native Americans, Euro American colonists, and African Americans." One of the reasons why early evidence of crab consumption is difficult to uncover is because the blue crab carapace is more fragile than oyster shells, so it deteriorates more rapidly over time. The crab shell pieces have often not been recognized during archaeological digs.

Despite this murky past, we do know that by the 1800s, crabs were a fairly common meal. So plentiful were they that crabs were often served as free bar snacks to lure patrons in to buy beer. This gave rise to bar owners concocting their own spicy coatings to put on the crabs, both to add flavor and to create thirst. In an age when one can pay as much as $100 per dozen, it's surprising to think that they were once given away.

Blue's Anatomy

The Chesapeake blue crab, *Callinectes sapidus*, is smaller than other popular varieties like the Dungeness or Alaskan king crabs. They are blue-gray in color, except for the claws (also called chelipeds) of the females which are red-tipped, like painted fingernails. Females are also distinguishable from males by the shape of their abdominal apron. Immature females, or "she-crabs," have a triangular apron. Once the females are fully mature, the apron becomes more rounded like a Byzantine dome. The male apron is shaped a bit like . . . well, a skinny penis. (Or, for family audiences, an inverted "T.") This is not coincidental as the male crab's genitalia, or pleopods, are located under the tip of this apron. If you've ever eaten steamed crabs, you've definitely seen the antennae-like things pop out once the apron has been lifted.

Speaking of genitalia, we might as well get right into it. The mating ritual of blue crabs is quite elaborate. When a male crab spots a female crab of his liking, flashing those red chelipeds seductively, he does a little balletic dance on the tips of his walking legs. He then extends his claws and waves them about before kicking up a storm of sand just to make sure she's paying attention. The female will also wave her arms about as she attempts

to position herself underneath the male. With this assurance that she is receptive, the male cradles the female and carries her off to a place where they can mate. The journey can take anywhere from two days to a week. Once the proper location is found (usually a spot abundant with eelgrass), the female begins to molt her shell while the male stands guard over her.

Molting is a draining process, so the male will wait by patiently as the female takes in water to replenish her muscles. When the female is ready, she will flip onto her back and the male will mount her in a position quite familiar to humans. The female opens two pores on her apron into which the male inserts his pleopods. After several hours, the mating ritual is completed, but the male will still carry the female around underneath him for a couple more days until her new shell is fully hardened. They then go their separate ways as the female burrows underground for the winter. The sperm will be stored until the spring, at which time she fertilizes her eggs. And while a female crab mates only once, she can hold on to her eggs and produce multiple broods during her lifetime.

While female crabs molt as part of the mating process, generally, molting is an ongoing process for both sexes. Blue crabs will shed their old shells over a dozen times during their brief life spans, providing another culinary opportunity for those who love crabs. Soft-shell crabs are simply crabs whose new shell has not yet hardened. Because they have no sturdy carapace, they can be eaten whole, shell and all, without the trouble of picking that must occur with a steamed hard-shell crab.

Starting in the late nineteenth century, soft-shell crabs grew in popularity, soon rivaling that of Maryland's beloved oysters. Harvesting soft-shell crabs is a specialized industry that requires a trained eye. The signs of molting are pretty subtle. For example, about two weeks before molting, crabs will exhibit what is called the "white sign," or the first faint outline of the new shell forming under the old one. Watermen refer to these crabs as "snots" or "greens." If the crab shows a thin pink line on its backfin, the "pink sign," then it will molt in less than a week. A "red sign" crab is going to molt in two days. Finally, "rank peelers" will molt in hours.

When crabs show physical signs that they are about to molt, watermen hold them in shallow tubs known as floats where they can step out of their old shell. At this point they are called "peelers" or "busters," and are removed from the water to stop the hardening of their new shell. If peelers are allowed to stay in the water, within twelve hours they go from soft-shells to "papershells," and in twenty-four hours their new shells are rather leathery. These crabs are called "buckrams," and are unmarketable as soft crabs. They're still tasty, however, if a bit crunchy, when battered and fried.

Battering and frying is one of the most common ways to cook soft crabs. Often the fried crabs are just slapped between two slices of white bread and consumed with gusto. As children, it was always a bit disconcerting to see our parents devouring a sandwich that had legs sticking out of the sides, as if it contained a deep fried tarantula.

Hard Habit to Break

The season for fresh soft-shells is usually limited to the spring, but hard-shell crabs are enjoyed throughout the summer and into early fall. Crab feasts in

Maryland are as important to summer fun as clambakes in New England or crab boils in Louisiana. It's not just a meal but an opportunity for family and friends to spend happy hours together while eating and imbibing large quantities of beer. The act of cracking open a crab and extracting every bit of its meat is a time-consuming process, so it's best to spend that time surrounded by people with whom you want to share stories and have some laughs. Beer goes great with spicy crabs and doesn't exactly hurt the conversation either.

There are numerous crab houses around Maryland where you can sit down to a large table covered in butcher paper and let the staff do all the steaming and cleaning up afterward. Still other places sell steamed crabs for takeout so you can rip through a pile of crabs in the privacy of your own home or backyard. Those who want the full crab feast experience will steam the crabs at home.

Steaming is a relatively easy process but not for the squeamish. You have to start with live blue crabs and steam them the very same day. Make sure you do not use dead crabs. Fill a large pot with equal parts water and vinegar or beer so that the mixture covers the bottom about an inch deep. Bring the liquid to a boil and put in a steamer tray that sits above the liquid. Using a pair of tongs, layer your crabs on the steamer tray, belly side down, and coat them with a healthy sprinkling of Old Bay® Seasoning. Some people feel it's more humane to turn the crab on its belly and stick a knife through the shell

Crabs + beer — few combinations are better

The prize of the backfin.

Scraping off the dead man's fingers

Cracking open the body

© Kathy Wielech Patterson

behind the mouth before putting them in the pot; however, crabs are pretty feisty creatures with claws that can do some damage, so this procedure requires skill. It's easier to grab them with tongs and drop them into the pot, but be prepared for some unnerving scratching sounds.

Once the crabs are layered on the steamer tray and covered with seasoning, cover the pot and bring the liquid back up to a boil. Then steam the crabs for 20 to 30 minutes, at which time they will have lost their blue/gray hue and turned a bright red. After you remove the crabs from the pot, sprinkle them with additional Old Bay® Seasoning. Those babies should be spicy! If you are cooking a large number of crabs, like a bushel full, you will have to cook them in batches. Be sure to replenish the steaming liquid periodically or you will have a nasty smelling mess on your hands.

Have you ever noticed, when eating hard crabs, that once in a while you get a big crab that seems lightweight and doesn't have much meat on the inside? These crabs are known as "skinnies," "white bellies," "whities," "snowballs," or any number of other terms. When a crab finishes molting into its shiny new shell, it's about one-third larger than it was before the molt. But only on the outside. On the inside, the crab is still puny and needs to pump up to fit the new exoskeleton. By the time it fills out, the shell is no longer bright white on the belly, but has an aged appearance and perhaps some rusty-looking stains. If you're able to catch your own crabs, throw the whiteys back and keep the "old" ones for the cooking pot.

After cooking comes the fun part—the eating. When it comes to picking crabs, there are two schools of thought—one involves removing the legs before cleaning and the other does not. We like to remove the legs, since any meat that comes off with them is that much less we have to dig for later. Don't just yank them out—grab a leg up high near the body and bend it downward. You should hear a small snap as it breaks away from the shell. Use a little finesse to gently wiggle the leg away from the body; hopefully there will be a hunk of meat attached to it. In the case of the backfin, there will be quite a bit of meat. If not, all is not lost—the meat is still inside. All crabs are different, so you won't get lucky every time.

Next, turn the crab so it's belly-up. Using a short, non-serrated knife, lift up the slim, pointed tip of the flap-like apron (which is much larger on the female) and pull it upward until it's perpendicular to the body of the crab. At this point, you should be able to slide the tip of the knife within the newly revealed gap between the bottom and top shells. Twist the knife and the halves should separate easily; remove the top shell.

© Jay Flemi

What you have left will be pretty ugly, but stay with it! Use your knife or fingers to scrape off the gills or "dead man's fingers" from both sides of the body, and remove the squiggly mess of guts in the center. What you'll have left is two halves of the body, joined by a thin piece of shell. With one half in each hand, bring them toward each other to crack the shell and separate the halves.

Using the knife or your fingers, remove the meat from the various chambers that make up the crab's body. The shell is quite easy to break with a little pressure, but the going might be slow until you get the hang of it.

When you've exhausted the supply of meat within the body, move onto the claws (the legs aren't really worth bothering with). Bend each "elbow" the wrong direction to separate the top and bottom pieces of the claw. Grab the edges of the pincer (watch out—they're sharp) and pull them apart. You should be able to wiggle the "thumb" portion of the pincer away from the shell, hopefully pulling out a piece of cartilage and a chunk of meat. If you only get part of it, use your hammer to crack the shell and remove it the hard way. Use the hammer on the white portion of the bottom part of the claw to crack it in the same way. Some people like to place the blade edge of their knife against the shell and hammer that, instead, which can make a cleaner break.

Crabsody in Blue

While devouring steamed crabs has been a Maryland ritual for generations, these days, the crabs that are sprawled out on the dining table are just as likely to come from sources other than the Chesapeake. With the Bay's crustacean populations dwindling since the 1990s, many crabs are imported from the Carolinas or the Gulf of Mexico to satisfy our cravings. Numerous reasons have been cited for the decline, including pollution and climate change. Warmer waters, changing currents, and excess amounts of nitrogen and phosphorus in the water create less hospitable living areas for crabs. A rise in temperature prohibits reproduction, and nitrogen and phosphorus causes algae blooms that inhibit the growth of the vegetal matter and small organisms crabs eat to survive.

With declining populations, the harvesting of crabs has been curtailed in recent years. While overfishing is only one part of the problem, controlling the number of crabs harvested each year is the only way to preserve a sustainable population. Each year, the Maryland Department of Natural Resources (DNR) conducts a winter dredge survey that estimates the number of crabs in the Maryland section of the Bay; a similar survey is also conducted in Virginia. By visiting 1,550 sites and using metal dredges to pull up crabs wintering in the mud, the DNR is able to determine the number of crabs estimated to inhabit the waters. These numbers are used to determine the target level of fishing pressure that can be permitted while preserving a healthy crab population. With one-third of the nation's blue crab catch coming from the Chesapeake Bay, maintaining an adequate number of reproducing adults is critical.

The good news is that blue crabs have seemed to show a bit of a rebound in recent years. The 2015 winter dredge survey estimated that 411 million blue crabs were living in the Bay, a 38 percent increase from 2014. There were also 101 million adult female crabs, significantly higher than the 68.5

million in 2013. Of course, efforts to improve water quality and control harvesting must remain vigilant if this increase is to continue.

Blue crabs are harvested by any number of ways. Most are caught in crab pots, wire cages with bait inside, a development of the 1920s. Crabs wander in to eat the bait and then find that they can't get out again. Crabs don't learn from the mistakes of others, so a crab pot may be rather full when a waterman checks in on it. Generally, a waterman has many pots, each marked with an identifying float. He checks them daily, removing and sorting his catch, replenishing bait, then dropping them back into the water for more. Other watermen work trotlines, long fishing lines, anchored on both ends, that are dropped to the bottom of a body of water. Bait is attached to the line at intervals, either with simple knots or shorter lines called "snoods." Crabbers run one or more lines up to a mile long and work them from a boat. Salted eel is a favorite bait, but trash fish or bits of meat like bull lips (mmm, bull lips) works, too. But not chicken necks. Oh, chicken necks are terrific bait for catching blue crabs, but you'll not likely catch a career waterman using them. In fact, "chicken-neckers" is a popular derogatory term used by watermen to describe amateurs. They seem to think it's an insult. We amateurs still use 'em. They work, don't they?

Watermen are a special breed. Many have descended from generations of men who have worked the waters, so crabbing is in their blood. The majority are independent businessmen who own their boats and equipment, and if they can't get out on the water and have a decent catch, they don't make money. And the work is hard, physical labor. But most watermen love their jobs and do it for as many years as their health allows.

Because they've spent so many years observing, watermen have an intimate knowledge of what goes on in the life of a blue crab. They can fairly accurately determine how well a harvest will go, as well as when crabs are ready to molt. So it's not surprising that they don't take lightly to any new regulations that come about. For instance, in order to leave more female crabs in the water that can mate and spawn, both the legal size of peeler crabs and the months in which they are harvestable were changed in 2015. Normally, it was to pull out female crabs measuring only 3¼ inches early in the season that starts April 1; the new requirement was that they be 3½ inches, which used to apply only after July 14. As the smaller crabs make up a goodly portion of the crabbers' income, this is a big loss for the folks who rely on the soft shell industry. It's serious and life-affecting—for both crabbers and crabs.

Sadly, the sustainability of crabs can only be controlled by regulating the size and number of crustaceans that can be harvested. Some years the crabs are affected by the watermen, and in others, the watermen are affected by regulations. A shame there isn't blue crab aquaculture.

Or is there?

Crab in a Lab

Callinectes sapidus isn't the only over-fished crab in the world. Over in Japan, low numbers of the stock of *Portunus trituberculatus*, a species of swimming crab, led to a hatchery-based stock replenishment program in which millions of juveniles were introduced into depleted waters. This was back in the 1970s . . . so why hasn't a similar program been initiated for the Chesapeake Bay?

It's complicated. The University of Maryland Biotechnology Institute's Center of Marine Biotechnology started a project in 2000 to determine whether they could successfully culture our beloved blue crab. With the help of Maryland Senator Barbara Mikulski, who earmarked federal funding for the project, a grant from Phillips Foods, and some state money, the project proved successful. But the number of crabs produced in the lab so far hasn't been enough to compensate for the number of wild crabs harvested each year. And funding has disappeared for the UMBC project, so a hatchery large enough to produce the tens of millions of young crabs that would be needed to replenish the Bay is not possible at this time. However, neither red tape nor lack of funding can refute the fact that crab aquaculture is a possible reality for the future.

The Future of Chesapeake Products —
Yoni Zohar

There have been those who pooh-pooh the viability of culturing blue crabs, but Yonathan Zohar isn't one of them. In fact, he's been at the forefront of crab aquaculture research for over fifteen years now. As director of the Center of Marine Biotechnology at the University of Maryland Biotechnology Institute, Zohar has examined the minutiae of crab biology and developed a method of creating lab-grown crustaceans that behave much as wild-born examples of *Callinectes sapidus* do.

In order to do this, Zohar studied the reproductive endocrinology of crabs, which he likens to being an OB/GYN. Part psychologist, too, as he has determined that stress is a primary factor for sea creatures having issues with reproducing in captivity. Rather than tinker with crab genetics, Zohar and his team manipulate the environment. The scientists work with sooks, or fertilized female crabs, supplied by local watermen. To get them to release their fertilized eggs in the lab, scientists use a technique called photoperiod manipulation to alter the amount of light exposure they receive per day, along with the temperature and salinity of the water the crabs are kept in. They are put in cold water, low-light conditions to simulate winter before being subjected to an artificial spring with warmer, saltier waters and more light. Once the sooks believe they are in the waters of the lower Bay, their normal spawning ground, they release some of their eggs. Yes, not all . . . another thing that the team learned about crabs is that females, once fertilized, can hold onto their eggs for a length of time and release them in batches. In fact, a female crab can produce up to five broods in the same season, one every couple of weeks.

The eggs hatch into larvae, which go through eight distinct stages, each requiring a special diet of various algae and microscopic animals, all of which must also be grown in the lab. When the larval stages are over, the little crabs have legs and look much like adults. And like adult crabs, they molt. While soft, they are prime candidates to be eaten by their brethren and sistren, so the scientists distract them from each other with more food and places to hide from each other.

Once the crablings that survive the cannibalistic stage are two months old, they are large enough (two-thirds of an inch!) to be released into the wild after being tagged with wee bits of magnetic wire. So far, hundreds of thousands of crabs have gone from the hatchery to the water, but to really make a difference in the Bay's crab population, the project needs to be scaled up considerably, into the millions. Right now, Maryland doesn't have that money, nor are federal dollars available. Considering that the blue crab is one of the most valuable fisheries in Maryland (and also in the states of Virginia and North Carolina), it seems a bit foolhardy not to pursue crab aquaculture with some urgency, especially since the technology has been around for over a decade already.

Yoni Zohar is not one to rest on his laurels. While he'd love to establish a centralized blue crab hatchery in Maryland, right now the funding for such things is coming from states around the Gulf of Mexico where blue crab constitutes an important fishery. In addition to taking his crab aquaculture findings south, he's also working on what he calls the "holy grail" of aquaculture, the bluefin tuna. This overfished favorite of sushi eaters the world over poses its own set of problems to aquaculturists, but we won't be surprised when it becomes another Zohar success story.

Smith Island

Known for its crabs, hospitality, and Maryland's official dessert, Smith Island is a census designated place in Somerset County, Maryland. Actually comprised of several small islands, Smith Island is located just below the halfway point of the Chesapeake Bay, at the border of Virginia. It's about twelve miles west of Crisfield, and only accessible by boat. Though Captain John Smith discovered the small archipelago in 1608 and named it the Russell Isles, Smith Island took its current name from Henry Smith of Jamestown, who owned a portion of the Island's 9.2 total square miles.

According to the 2010 Census, Smith Island has 276 residents (down nearly a hundred from the 364 people recorded ten years prior) who live in and around three villages of Tylerton, Ewell, and Rhodes Point. Although population numbers are down, most native islanders can still boast a lineage that can be traced back a dozen or more generations to the area's original seventeenth-century settlers from Wales and England's southwestern-most counties of Dorset and Cornwall. Indeed, it has often been said that the unique dialect spoken on Smith Island is very much like the dialects of the West Country.

Smith Island was originally settled as a grazing land for livestock, but by the 1800s, the crab and oyster industries were king. Eventually, with the depletion of oyster stock in the Bay, crabbing became the predominant industry. Today, it is a hub for Maryland's soft shell crab industry.

© Bettina Perry

In 2008, Smith Island cake was declared the official dessert of the state of Maryland. While the multi-layer treat has apparently been made for generations on Smith Island, nobody is quite sure of its origin. The seven-layer Dobos torte, created in Hungary in 1884, is similar. It's said that Smith Island's pride and joy started as a normal three- or four-layer cake, and competitive local bakers tried to outdo each other by adding more and more layers. Normally, a Smith Island cake will have at least eight layers and as many as twelve, suggesting that culinary one-upmanship has been alive and well in the Chesapeake Bay. The traditional cake is yellow with chocolate frosting, but these days one will find variations in flavors like lemon and red velvet, and recipes that include crushed candy bars sprinkled between the layers as well.

Smith Island Cake

According to several online sources, the recipe we have adapted here comes from Frances Kitching, a Smith Island resident renowned for her culinary ability. However, it does not appear in *Mrs. Kitching's Smith Island Cookbook.*

If you don't have ten round cake pans, nor want to make the investment, you can make the cake with as few pans as you have. Remember to thoroughly wash, dry, and re-grease them before reusing. Resist the urge to use parchment, as peeling parchment off such thin layers might cause them to tear.

For the cake:

3 cups flour

¼ teaspoon salt

1 heaping teaspoon baking powder

2 cups sugar

8 ounces unsalted butter, softened

5 large eggs

1 cup evaporated milk

2 teaspoons vanilla

For the frosting:

8 ounces butter, softened

2 (12-ounce) cans evaporated milk

8 heaping tablespoons unsweetened cocoa powder

2 pounds confectioner's sugar

To make the cake: Preheat oven to 350°F. Lightly grease ten 9-inch round baking pans.

Sift together flour, salt, and baking powder. Using a stand mixer, cream together sugar and butter. Add eggs one at a time, beating until smooth after each addition. Beat in flour mixture a little at a time.

Combine the evaporated milk with ½ cup water and the vanilla and drizzle into the batter while the mixer is still running. Mix until just combined.

Pour about ¾ cup of batter into each of the prepared baking pans, spreading evenly. Place pans on the middle oven rack, two or three at a time, and bake for 10 to 15 minutes, or until a toothpick inserted into the center of the cake comes out clean.

Allow the layers to cool slightly before turning them out of the pans onto cooling racks. The layers are fragile and may tear; once iced, however, no one will notice.

To make the frosting: In a large saucepan, melt the butter. Remove the pan from the heat and whisk in the evaporated milk. Whisk in the cocoa powder, then return the pan to the heat. Cook for 10 minutes over low heat, making sure the mixture does not boil or burn.

Remove pan from heat and slowly whisk in the confectioner's sugar. Put back over low heat once more and cook slowly, until thickened, about 45 minutes. The mixture should form a ribbon when drizzled from a spoon.

To assemble the cake: Place one cooled layer on a cake plate. Spread with two or three tablespoons of warm icing, then top with the next layer. Continue in this manner until all ten cake layers have been stacked. Cover the top and sides of the cake with the remainder of the icing. If the icing slides off the cake too readily, allow it to cool a bit before proceeding.

Ten-Layer Yellow Cake with Chocolate Cream Cheese Frosting, Salty Pretzel Crumbs, and Raspberries

COURTESY OF CHEF BETTINA PERRY

This cake borrows heavily from what might be considered a "Milk Bar"-style cake, popularized by James Beard Award–winning pastry chef Christina Tosi. This type of layer cake does not have frosting around the sides, and there is usually some sort of textural component in addition to the cake and the frosting. Baltimore-area pastry chef Bettina Perry took the classic Smith Island cake flavors of yellow cake with sweet chocolate frosting and added the tanginess of raspberry, the salty zing and texture of pretzels, and tossed in a little candy as well. This is in keeping with more modern versions of Smith Island cake that are gussied up with crushed candy bars.

You can build this cake free-form, as a Smith Island cake would be, or you can get a little fussier and purchase a 9-inch cake ring that is 2 inches high and some 4-inch acetate cake collars to form a mold of sorts. The technique is described below, at the end of the recipe.

For the cake:

3 cups flour

¼ teaspoon salt

1 heaping teaspoon baking powder

2 cups sugar

8 ounces unsalted butter, softened

5 eggs

1 cup evaporated milk

2 teaspoons vanilla

1 (12-ounce) bag miniature chocolate chips

1 (8-ounce) bag toffee bits

For the pretzel crumbs:

1 pound bag of pretzels

1 cup confectioner's sugar

½ cup all-purpose flour

1 tablespoon kosher salt

4 ounces unsalted butter

2 large eggs

For the frosting:

9 cups confectioner's sugar

1½ cups cocoa powder

3 (8-ounce) packages cream cheese, softened

12 ounces unsalted butter, softened

1 teaspoon salt

3 tablespoons vanilla extract

To assemble:

1 jar seedless raspberry preserves

Fresh raspberries

To make the cake: Preheat oven to 350°F. Lightly grease as many 9-inch round baking pans as you have.

Sift together flour, salt, and baking powder. Using a stand mixer, cream together sugar and butter. Add eggs one at a time, beating until smooth after each addition. Beat in flour mixture a little at a time.

Combine the evaporated milk with ½ cup water and the vanilla and drizzle into the batter while the mixer is still running. Mix until just combined.

Pour about ¾ cup of batter into each of the prepared baking pans and sprinkle with 3 tablespoons of chocolate chips and 2 tablespoons of toffee bits. Bake layers for 16 to 18 minutes. Allow the layers to cool slightly before turning them out of the pans onto cooling racks. This can be done a day ahead, especially if you are limited in the number of pans you own and can only bake two at a time.

To make pretzel crumbs: Preheat oven to 350°F.

Lightly pulse the pretzels in a food processor until it resembles a chunky "dust." You'll need three cups of the dust for this recipe.

Pour pretzel dust into the bowl of a stand mixer fitted with the paddle attachment. Add the remaining ingredients and mix on medium speed until a dough forms.

Using your hands, crumble the dough into chunks on one or two cookie sheets. Bake pans for 15 to 18 minutes. The dough will probably have merged into one big cookie. When cooled, break the cookie up into various textures, from bite-sized crumbs to both coarse and fine sand. Set aside until ready to use.

To make frosting: Sift together the confectioner's sugar and cocoa powder.

Place the cream cheese and butter in the bowl of a stand mixer fitted with the paddle attachment. Cream them until light and fluffy, then add the cocoa/sugar mixture slowly, cup by cup, until it's all incorporated, scraping down the bowl as necessary. Stir in the salt and vanilla. Turn speed to high and beat frosting for 2 minutes. Set aside until ready to use.

To assemble the cake free form: Place a cake layer on a 10-inch cardboard cake round or serving plate. Spread a thin layer of raspberry jam on the cake. Spread a layer of the frosting (about one cup) on next, followed by a handful of the pretzel crumbs. Repeat layers until all cake is used. Coat the top layer with jam but not frosting. Decorate with handfuls of pretzel crumbs and fresh raspberries.

To assemble the cake with a cake collar and acetate: Place the cake ring on a 10-inch cardboard cake round. Line the ring with one strip of the acetate. Place the first layer of cake down into the ring. Spread a thin layer of raspberry jam on the cake. Spread a layer of the frosting (about 1 cup) on next, followed by a handful of the pretzel crumbs.

With your index finger, gently tuck a second strip of acetate between the cake ring and top quarter inch of the first ring of acetate, so you have a ring of acetate about six inches tall. Set a second layer of cake down onto the layer of pretzel crumbs on the previous layer, and repeat the layers of jam, frosting, and crumbs. You may need additional layers of acetate. Rather than tucking them in, tape them to the outside of the last acetate sheet.

Once the cake is complete, chill it for 12 hours. Three hours before serving, gently peel off the acetate and pop off the ring mold. The cake is best when served at room temperature.

The Spice of Life

It's hard to imagine eating Maryland seafood without the tongue-tingling blend of spices known the world over as Old Bay® Seasoning.

Back in pre–World War II Germany, Gustav Brunn was a successful spice merchant. That is, until the Nazis arrested him and sent him to the Buchenwald concentration camp in 1938. His family managed to bribe the Gestapo to secure his release, and they fled to the United States.

Brunn had an uncle in Baltimore, so they settled there, and Brunn began work at the McCormick Spice Company. That job lasted all of a few days; he believed he was fired either because he was Jewish, or because he didn't speak English. In either case, he eventually opened his own spice company, Baltimore Spice, which was conveniently located across from Baltimore's wholesale fish market. Seafood merchants would come in, looking for seasonings with which to steam their crabs. Brunn assembled a blend of mustard, celery seed, red pepper, bay leaves, cloves, allspice, ginger, mace, cardamom, cinnamon, paprika, and salt and pepper that he dubbed "India Girl." The name was later changed to "Old Bay," which made more sense, considering its primary use.

The Brunns sold Baltimore Spice in 1985, but not to McCormick, as Gustav never forgot the way he was treated there. Eventually McCormick managed to buy the Old Bay® brand from the new owner, keeping the famous formula and the iconic yellow, blue, and red can.

Though it's hard to imagine, Old Bay® Seasoning isn't the only crab seasoning in town. Around the same time period, post–World War II, James Ozzle Strigle and his wife, Dot, established J.O. Spice Company Inc. Strigle was born and raised on Tangier Island, Virginia, where seafood was life. As the story goes, he thought it would be a swell idea to take the spice recipes the island's watermen used for their seafood and package them for sale. The Strigles opened a storefront in Baltimore City, where they mixed their blends and sold them at the local wholesale fish market. The seasonings were popular, the business grew, and today the business, still family-owned, is one of a handful that gives Old Bay® Seasoning a bit of competition in the Delmarva region.

Crab Soups

It is not unusual to order a bowl of Maryland crab soup as an appetizer before tucking into a few dozen steamed hard crabs. The general consensus around here is always the more crab the merrier. Typically a vegetable soup studded with chunks and shreds of crab, a Maryland crab soup can have a beef, ham, or bacon base, and usually—but not always—contains tomatoes. While most modern Marylanders think of this version as the quintessential Maryland crab soup, a look through some old cookbooks reveals that cream of crab was probably first. This version is descended from French bisques and calls for milk or cream, but the modern penchant for thickening the broth with cornstarch or flour makes for something closer to wallpaper paste than to a delicate bisque. In any case, the two styles of Maryland crab soup are about as similar to each other as New England clam chowder is to Manhattan clam chowder.

© Kathy Wielech Patterson

Cream of Crab Soup

This recipe is adapted from the 1874 cookbook, *Queen of the Kitchen: A Collection of "Old Maryland" Family Receipts for Cooking,* by Miss Tyson. Unlike most modern recipes, this soup is all about the cream and the crab, without any distracting spices. Not even nutmeg, which was a popular addition to creamy dishes. The original recipe suggests letting the "soup boil for 20 minutes after adding the crabs," which would have reduced any crab lumps to mere shreds. Doing so would probably increase the crab flavor in the soup, but we don't recommend trying it unless you have a large supply of already broken-up crab meat on hand. (SERVES 6)

1 quart whole milk

1 tablespoon cold unsalted butter

1 tablespoon all-purpose flour

1 cup heavy cream

8 ounces crab meat (backfin, or a mix of lump and claw meat)

Salt and freshly ground pepper to taste

Bring milk to a boil. Make a beurre manie by kneading together the butter and flour into a smooth paste. Add it, a little at a time, to the boiling milk, stirring constantly. When soup is thick, turn down the heat and add the cream and the crab. Cook only until warmed through. Season with salt and pepper to taste.

Cream of Crab Soup with Garlic Confit and Avocado

COURTESY OF CHEF SCOTT HINES, B&O AMERICAN BRASSERIE

While rooted in tradition, the garlic confit gives Chef Hines' rendition of cream of crab soup a whole new dimension. Cooking garlic cloves slowly in oil makes them meltingly tender and sweet. While it might seem like a good idea to make a big batch of the stuff to keep on hand, for some reason, the garlic and oil combo promotes bacterial growth. To be on the safe side, just make as much as you'll need to use right away. If you do have any leftovers, keep them in a clean covered container in the fridge for no longer than one week. For this recipe, just divide the garlic evenly between the servings.
(SERVES 8)

For garlic confit:

2 heads garlic

Canola oil

For soup:

1 onion, cut into small dice

4 ounces unsalted butter

4 ounces all-purpose flour

1 quart whole milk

1 quart heavy cream

1 cup clam juice

¼ cup Old Bay® Seasoning

½ cup sherry

Freshly ground black pepper

2 pounds lump crabmeat

1 tablespoon each finely chopped herbs (parsley, chervil, tarragon, chives)

2 avocados, cut into medium dice

1 cup saltine crackers, chopped and toasted

To make confit: Separate the garlic into individual cloves and peel them. Place garlic in the smallest saucepan you have and pour over enough of the oil to cover by half an inch or so. Cook garlic very gently over low heat for about 40 minutes, until tender. Allow the garlic to cool in the oil before pouring it into a very clean covered container.

To make soup: In a large pot, cook the onion in the butter until softened. Add the flour, whisking to incorporate fully into a blonde roux. Whisking constantly, gradually pour in the milk, cream, and clam juice. Stir in the Old Bay® Seasoning and simmer for 20 minutes, stirring occasionally.

Stir in the sherry and season with black pepper.

Combine the herbs in a small bowl.

To serve: Place 4 ounces of crab meat into the bottom of a serving bowl. Ladle over some of the soup. Garnish with the herbs, avocado, garlic confit, and saltines.

Uncle Elmore's Maryland Crab Soup

COURTESY OF CHEF WINSTON BLICK, CLEMENTINE

Because there are as many versions of Maryland crab soup as there are cooks, and there's no one standardized style of broth, we're offering Winston Blick's family recipe as our classic recipe.

"My family came down definitively on one side of the crab soup debate. The debate consisted of whether to use tomato-based broth or beef-based broth. I'm gonna wade right in and say I'm not into tomato soup with vegetables and crabs. I like the interplay between beef broth, sweet corn, and tart tomatoes." Chef Blick also prefers to use claw meat in his soup, rather than the pricier lump crab. "The claw meat is the dark meat of the crab, with a sweeter, nuttier and more complex flavor. (Might be another argument here.)"

Winston also bucks what might be called tradition by calling for J.O. Spice Company crab spice. It's saltier than Old Bay® Seasoning, so if you decide to use the latter, you'll need more than the recipe calls for.

(SERVES 8–10)

4 cups diced ripe tomatoes

4 cups diced carrots

3 cups diced red potatoes

3 cups diced red onions

2 cloves garlic, minced

2 cups green beans, cut into ¼-inch pieces

1 cup diced green cabbage

¼ cup Worcestershire sauce

1 gallon beef broth

1 tablespoon coarse ground pepper

1–2 tablespoons J.O. Spice Company brand crab spice, to taste

2 pounds blue crab claw meat (divided use), picked over for shells

6 (or more) ears of corn, cooked, kernels cut off the cob

Put vegetables, Worcestershire, broth, pepper, one tablespoon of the crab spice, and one pound of the crabmeat in a 6-quart stockpot and bring to a simmer. Cook for 10 minutes and taste for salt, adding more of the crab spice if necessary. Add the corn and the second pound of crab and cook, covered, for another 10 to 15 minutes.

"You've just made Uncle Elmore's crab soup. Uncle Elmore knew his business. It's even better the next day."

Roasted Vegetable Gazpacho with Crab Salad

Nobody says that crab soup has to be served hot. This chilled version is full of flavor, and a perfect dish for steamy hot Maryland summers.
(SERVES 4–6)

For the soup:

3 pounds fresh tomatoes

¼ cup extra virgin olive oil

Salt and freshly ground pepper

2 red bell peppers

1 cucumber, peeled and cut into chunks

4 tablespoons red wine vinegar

4 teaspoons Old Bay® Seasoning

1 teaspoon light brown sugar

© Kathy Wielech Patterson

For the salad:

1 tablespoon orange juice

1 teaspoon fresh lime juice

Pinch Old Bay® Seasoning

½ cup cooked fresh corn kernels

¼ cup cooked edamame

1 scallion, white and green part very thinly sliced

½ pound fresh backfin crabmeat, picked over for shells

To make the soup: Preheat oven to 400°F. Core the tomatoes and cut them in half. Scoop out the seeds and juice and reserve. Place tomatoes on a foil-lined baking sheet and drizzle with half the olive oil. Season with salt and black pepper. Cut red peppers into quarters, removing stems and seeds. Place pepper pieces, skin side-up, on a separate foil-lined baking sheet. Drizzle with remaining olive oil; season with salt and black pepper. Place vegetables in the oven and roast for 45 minutes, until vegetables are soft and skins begin to blacken in spots. Remove trays from oven and cool vegetables to room temperature. Remove one tablespoon of oil from the pan of peppers and reserve for the salad.

Once veggies are cool, place them and any accompanying juices in a blender along with the reserved tomato seeds and juice. Add the cucumber and puree until smooth. You may need to do this in batches; if this is the case, combine them in a large bowl or pitcher before adding the remaining ingredients. Stir in the vinegar, Old Bay® Seasoning, and the brown sugar. Season with salt and pepper to taste. Refrigerate until very cold.

To make the salad: In a large bowl, combine the reserved roasted red pepper oil, the orange and lime juices, and a generous pinch of Old Bay® Seasoning. Whisk together with a fork. Stir in the corn, edamame, and scallion. Add the crab and fold gently to coat with the dressing, being careful not to break up the crab too much.

Before serving, taste soup for seasoning and re-season with more Old Bay® Seasoning or salt to taste. Ladle chilled soup into shallow bowls. Divide crab salad into equal portions, placing a mound of it into the center of each bowl. Sprinkle with additional Old Bay® Seasoning.

Spicy Crab and Sausage Soup

In this relatively fast and easy version, we use sausage to flavor the broth. We recommend a fresh Mexican-chorizo-type sausage, rather than a cured Spanish chorizo. If you have partial bags of veggies in the freezer, this is a good way to use them up. And if you're not a fan of lima beans, don't worry, edamame makes a good substitute.

(SERVES 6–10)

1 medium onion, chopped

1 bunch scallions, chopped

2 teaspoons olive oil

3 Mexican-chorizo-style sausages (we like Johnsonville)

2 (15-ounce) cans diced tomatoes and their juices

1 tablespoon crab spice (we like Phillips® Seafood Seasoning for this dish)

1 teaspoon kosher salt

½ teaspoon finely ground black pepper

¼ teaspoon smoked paprika

Pinch cayenne pepper

1 cup fresh or frozen corn kernels

1 cup fresh or frozen peas

1 cup frozen lima beans or edamame

2 cups frozen green beans

1 pound crab meat from both body and claw, picked over for shells

In a deep pot, saute the onions and scallions in the olive oil over medium heat until softened, about 5 minutes. While that's cooking, skin and slice the sausages. Add them to the pot. Cook for 8 to 10 minutes, stirring frequently and breaking up the sausage into smaller chunks. Add the tomatoes and two cans of water.

Turn up the heat to bring the soup to a boil, then turn down to simmer. Cook 15 to 20 minutes. Add the seasonings and the vegetables and cook for another 10 minutes. Stir in the crab and serve hot.

Soft Shell Crabs

Soft shell crabs don't need much fuss. Clip off the face and apron, pull out the "dead man's fingers," and give the crabs a pan fry in a little butter, with or without dusting them with a bit of flour, first. Oh yes—clipping off the face is a crucial first step in preparing soft shell crabs. It's best to use kitchen shears for the job rather than a knife, but if you're squeamish about the whole thing, you can get your fishmonger to do it for you. Keep your prepared crabs cold and cook them as soon as you get them home, because they are best when they're fresh.

Chili-Lime Soft Shell Crabs

COURTESY OF CHEF MIKE RANSOM, B & O AMERICAN BRASSERIE

The usual method of cooking soft shells is to fry them crisp. Chef Ransom takes a different approach and braises the crabs in a flavored butter first, infusing them with juiciness and tons of flavor. He serves the crabs with a tangy tomato relish and a potato and leek combo meant to evoke a potato salad; it can be served warm, at room temperature, or even chilled.

Dehydrated corn can be purchased in some supermarkets (the Just Corn brand) or online at Nuts.com. It adds a little crunch to the dish as well as another layer of traditional Maryland flavor. The *Gochugaru* (Korean red pepper flakes) can be purchased at Asian markets or online. A quarter cup seems like a lot, but it's not nearly as spicy as cayenne or the crushed red pepper flakes one might normally use. If you do use standard red pepper flakes, just add a couple of teaspoons.

(MAKES 8 SERVINGS)

For the chili-lime butter:

Zest and juice of 2 limes

4 ounces lemon juice

1 tablespoon Vietnamese fish sauce

1 tablespoon kosher salt

1 pound unsalted butter, softened

¼ cup coarse ground Gochugaru

For tomato relish:

1 green tomato

1 yellow tomato

Zest and juice of 1 lime

1 tablespoon white wine vinegar

2 tablespoons extra virgin olive oil

1 teaspoon honey

Leaves from 1 sprig fresh tarragon

Salt and pepper to taste

5 ounces of baby arugula

For potatoes:

1 quart leeks

¼ cup extra virgin olive oil

2 teaspoons kosher salt

2 pounds small red-skin potatoes

Chopped parsley

Salt and pepper

Jessica Lemmo

For the crabs:
16 soft shell crabs, cleaned
4 ounces white wine

To serve:
1 cup dehydrated corn kernels

To make butter: Combine lime, lemon, fish sauce, and salt. Place butter into the bowl of a food processor and whip until smooth. While the processor is running, slowly add the lime mixture, fully incorporating all liquid until emulsified. Stir in the Korean pepper. Scrape butter into a plastic container with a lid and set aside.

To make tomato relish: Bring two quarts of water to a boil. Cut a shallow x into the skin on the bottom of each tomato. Drop the tomatoes in the boiling water for about 30 seconds, then place them in a bowl of ice water. The skins should peel off easily. Halve tomatoes, scoop out the seeds, and cut the flesh into medium dice. Place cut tomatoes in a bowl. Whisk together the remaining ingredients and pour over the tomatoes. Season with salt and pepper to taste. Refrigerate for 30 minutes.

To make potatoes: Trim off and discard root end of leeks. Cut leeks in half lengthwise and slice into ¼-inch half-moons. Wash thoroughly to remove any sand or grit.

In a large saucepan, heat olive oil until shimmering. Add leeks and kosher salt and cook over medium heat for about 10 minutes, or until soft but still bright green in color. Remove leeks from pan and allow to cool.

Boil potatoes in salted water until fork tender. Place them in a bowl and crush lightly with the back of a spoon. Add the leeks and chopped parsley, and season with salt and pepper to taste.

To make crabs: Warm ½ cup of the chili-lime butter in a large saute pan with 2 ounces of white wine. Add half of the crabs and poach at a medium simmer for about 8 minutes. Remove crabs to a wire rack placed over a baking sheet to catch the drips. Repeat with remaining crabs.

Once all the crabs are poached, simmer the butter until thickened, whisking occasionally to keep the sauce from separating. Remove from the heat and keep warm.

Preheat grill to medium. Pat excess butter from crabs and grill for about 4 minutes per side, which will give the shells a bit of crispness. When shells turn from bluish-grey to red, move crabs to hotter side of the grill for a minute or 2. Be careful not to burn the legs or claws. If you don't have a grill, you can brush the crabs lightly with a little oil and sear them in a hot saute pan or grill pan.

To serve: Place a dollop of the potatoes on each of eight plates. Arrange two crabs on top of potatoes and spoon over some of the reduced chili-lime butter. Toss the tomato relish with the baby arugula and place a handful on the side of the crabs to finish the plate. Garnish with dehydrated corn.

Crispy Soft Shell Crabs with Corn and Barley Congee

COURTESY OF CHEF CYRUS KEEFER, BALTIMORE COUNTRY CLUB

This soft shell dish has a distinct Asian flair, using both *Kombu* and *Nori* seaweed, which can be purchased in Asian markets, some health food stores, and online. *Dashi* is a stock used in Japanese cooking. *Congee* is typically a porridge-like rice dish, but barley works just as well. Chef Keefer has served this dish with either roasted baby zucchini or fried mushrooms, but a smattering of chopped scallion is all you need.
(SERVES 6)

For corn dashi:

2–3 corncobs

1 Spanish onion

1 cup diced scallion

2 star anise

1 pinch saffron threads

1 teaspoon sugar

2 tablespoons white soy sauce

Pinch salt

1 small sheet of Kombu seaweed

For the congee:

1 tablespoon white soy sauce

1 cup pearl barley

4 cups white corn kernels

½ cup peeled and diced carrot

2 tablespoons diced yellow onion

1½ teaspoons minced shallot

2 teaspoons vegetable oil

White wine

1 quart plus 1 cup corn dashi

1 fresh sage leaf

½ teaspoon kosher salt

Pinch sugar

½ tablespoon julienned *Nori*

For the crab:

½ cup flour

½ cup yellow cornmeal

1 tablespoon instant dashi powder

6 soft shell crabs, cleaned

Oil for frying

To serve:

1 tablespoon chopped scallion

To make the dashi: Cut the kernels off the cobs and reserve for the congee. Peel the onion, cut in half, and grill on cut sides until lightly charred.

Place cobs, onion, and other ingredients in a pot with enough water to cover and bring to a near boil, removing the Kombu just before it starts to bubble hard. Turn down to a simmer and cook for 45 minutes. Strain stock and refrigerate until ready to use.

To make the congee: Bring two cups of water and the soy sauce to a boil in a 2-quart saucepan. Add the barley and cook for about 20 minutes, until barley is tender. Drain barley well, spread it out on a baking pan, and refrigerate until cold.

Cook the corn, carrot, onion, and shallot in the oil over low heat, stirring regularly, until tender, about 45 minutes. Turn the heat up to high and deglaze pan with a splash of white wine. Cook

© Cyrus Keefer

until wine has completely evaporated, then add the one cup of corn dashi, the sage, salt, and sugar. Simmer for 20 minutes, then puree in a blender until silky smooth.

Put the cooked and chilled barley and one quart of corn Dashi in a large pot and simmer over medium heat for about 1 hour and 15 minutes, until the barley is soft and porridge-like. Stir in the corn puree and nori.

To make crabs: Combine the flour, cornmeal, and dashi powder on a plate. Dredge each crab in the flour mixture.

Heat oil in a deep fryer to 365°F. Cook crabs for 1 to 2 minutes on each side until golden brown and crisp. Drain on paper towel–lined plate. You can also shallow fry the crabs, if you prefer. Heat about ½ inch of oil in a large pan or cast iron skillet. Fry the crabs for 2 to 3 minutes on both sides until browned and crisp. Drain on paper towel–lined plate.

To serve: Place some of the congee in a shallow bowl. Cut each crab in quarters and arrange in the center of the congee, legs-up. Garnish each plate with some of the chopped scallion.

Crab Cakes

We're going to go out on a limb and say that crab cakes are probably the most popular crab dish in the state of Maryland, even more so than steamed crabs. Most supermarkets in the state carry some sort of canned or fresh crab product, although if at all reasonably priced it is unlikely to be the meat of *Callinectes sapidus*. But talk about a convenience product! A pound of pre-picked crabmeat is indeed expensive, but think of all the work it saves picking a dozen or more crabs yourself.

According to *the* authority on Chesapeake Bay eats, John Shields, "the local American Indian tribes made the first crab cakes by steaming them over rocks, picking the meat and binding it with a tuber veg (like a sweet potato)." They then fried them in bear fat.

The term "crab cake" is a twentieth-century convention that started to appear in cookbooks and on menus in the 1930s. Earlier, they were called "patties," or "croquettes." A very early printed recipe for crab cakes, titled "to fry crabs," can be found in English Chef Robert May's 1660 book, *The Accomplisht Cook*. While quite different from modern recipes in that the crab is seasoned with almond paste and nutmeg, it calls for mixing crab meat with grated bread, salt, and egg yolks. The meat is then dropped by spoonfuls into a batter, after which it's fried in clarified butter. The resulting patties are then put atop a beurre blanc that contains more crab, and topped with orange slices and parsley. Sounds good, but it's perhaps a little fussy for today's tastes. And this being an English recipe, the crab meat used wouldn't have had quite the same succulence of our Maryland crab.

There's not one way to make a crab cake. Generally, there is binder, filler, and seasoning in addition to plenty of luscious meat. Jumbo or "colossal" lump crab is often found listed on restaurant menus, but there's absolutely nothing wrong with a good old-fashioned cake made with backfin and even claw meat. Binder can be mayonnaise and/or egg; some antique recipes call for heavy cream or white sauce. Bread or cracker crumbs, even panko, can be a filler, although some locals insist that nothing at all should be added beyond binder and spices. As for seasoning, the widely available Old Bay® Seasoning is probably the best known, but companies like J.O. Spice Company Inc., Phillips® Seafood Seasoning, and Vann's Spices also make mighty fine versions.

Classic Crab Cakes

(SERVES 2–4)

1 egg

3 tablespoons mayonnaise

1 tablespoon Dijon mustard

1 teaspoon Worcestershire sauce

10 saltine crackers, crushed

2 teaspoons Old Bay® Seasoning

1 tablespoon finely chopped parsley

1 pound backfin crab meat, picked over for shells

Vegetable oil, for frying

In a bowl, beat egg into mayonnaise. Stir in mustard and Worcestershire, then add crackers, seasoning, and parsley. Gently fold in crab meat. Form into four patties.

Heat a few tablespoons of vegetable oil in a skillet. Cook crab cakes until golden brown on all sides. Serve with tartar sauce.

Crab Cakes à la Robert May

Our interpretation of Robert May's fried crab is a bit simpler than the original. The almond paste and batter are gone, but we kept the orange butter sauce (which is also tasty over any sort of broiled or pan-fried fish).

(SERVES 4)

For crab cakes:

1 large egg

¼ cup mayonnaise

1 tablespoon orange juice

1 teaspoon Dijon mustard

⅛ teaspoon freshly grated nutmeg

1 tablespoon chopped parsley

½ teaspoon salt

1 pound lump crabmeat, picked over for shells

1 cup fresh bread crumbs

Vegetable oil for frying

For orange beurre blanc:

2 tablespoons finely minced shallot

4 ounces neutral beer (we like Flying Dog Dead Rise for this recipe, or Blue Moon)

4 ounces orange juice

5 tablespoons heavy cream

10 tablespoons cold unsalted butter, cut into small pieces

1 tablespoon finely grated orange zest

Salt and white pepper, to taste

4 ounces crab meat, picked over for shells

To serve:

Chopped parsley

Lemon

© Kathy Wielech Patterson

To make crab cakes: Beat egg into the mayonnaise. Stir in orange juice, mustard, nutmeg, parsley, and salt. Gently fold in crabmeat, then fold in breadcrumbs. Form mixture into 8 patties. Put cakes on a plate, cover with plastic wrap, and refrigerate for at least 1 and up to 3 hours.

Heat a tablespoon of oil in a large nonstick skillet over medium heat. Add as many crab cakes as fit comfortably. Cook until golden brown on bottoms, about 4 minutes. Flip cakes and cook until the other side is browned. Drain cakes on paper towel–lined plates. Add more oil to skillet before cooking remaining crab cakes. (If you're cooking in batches, loosely tent plated cakes with aluminum foil to keep them warm until the rest are finished.)

To make beurre blanc: Add shallots to white wine and orange juice in a non-reactive saucepan. Boil over high heat and reduce to 2 to 3 tablespoons, about 5 minutes. Add cream and bring back to a boil. Once liquid starts to bubble, turn heat to low. Add butter, a couple small pieces at a time, whisking constantly. Don't add more butter until the previous pieces have been fully incorporated. Continue whisking in butter until the mixture is fully emulsified. If the heat seems too high, lift pan off the burner while whisking.

Stir in zest and season with salt and pepper to taste. Stir in crab and keep sauce warm until ready to serve.

To serve: Place a puddle of the orange beurre blanc on each of four plates and top with two crab cakes. Sprinkle with parsley and butter.

Mixed Cabbage Slaw

Just about everyone will tell you that the best accompaniment for a crab cake is a bowl of fresh cole slaw. This one is pretty and colorful and has the additional tang and crunch of Granny Smith apple.

(SERVES 6–8)

1 pint Brussels sprouts

2 cups loosely packed baby kale, stems removed

1 Granny Smith apple

2 teaspoons fresh lemon juice

2 cups finely shredded green cabbage

1 cup finely shredded red cabbage

1 large carrot, shredded

2 tablespoons apple cider vinegar

2 tablespoons sugar

½ cup mayonnaise

3 tablespoons full-fat Greek yogurt

1 teaspoon celery seed

½ teaspoon onion powder

2 teaspoons kosher salt

Freshly ground pepper

Trim stems and outer leaves from Brussels sprouts. Cut them in half and make a v-shaped cut into the stem end to remove as much of it as possible. Slice the leafy part of the sprouts thinly to shred them. Place in a large bowl.

Take several kale leaves and stack them. Roll the stacks into a cigar shape, then slice them crosswise to make thin ribbons. Repeat for all of the kale leaves. Add sliced kale to the bowl of Brussels sprouts.

Peel and core the apple. Cut the apple into matchstick-sized pieces. Toss with the lemon juice and add to the kale and sprouts. Add the green and red cabbage and carrot to the same bowl, tossing to combine.

In another bowl, combine the vinegar and sugar, stirring well to dissolve the sugar. Add the mayo, yogurt, celery seed, onion powder, and salt. Stir well. Pour dressing over vegetables and toss well to coat. Check seasoning and add more salt, pepper, and sugar to taste.

Classic Crab Imperial

For many years, the best way to fancy up a steak or plain fish was to top it with crab imperial. A ramekin of the mayonnaise-rich crab concoction topped with more mayo and broiled makes a mighty fine meal unto itself.
(SERVES 8)

1 small red bell pepper, diced

2 tablespoons unsalted butter

1 teaspoon flour

¼ cup milk

1 teaspoon Old Bay® Seasoning

4 tablespoons mayonnaise (divided use)

1 pound backfin crabmeat, picked over for shells

1 egg

Paprika

Preheat oven to 350°F.

Cook the bell pepper in the butter over medium heat until softened, 8 to 10 minutes. Sprinkle over the flour and stir well to combine. Pour in the milk and mix well to form a smooth paste. Remove from the heat and set aside to cool.

In a large bowl, stir together the Old Bay® Seasoning and 1 tablespoon of the mayonnaise. Gently fold in the crab. Pack the crab into 8 shallow ovenproof ramekins, or, even better, the cleaned shells from 8 steamed hard crabs.

In another bowl, beat the egg and three tablespoons mayonnaise together. Spread the mixture over the crabmeat in the ramekins/shells. Dust tops with paprika, then place ramekins onto a baking sheet. Bake for approximately 15 minutes, or until topping is browned and bubbly.

Chesapeake Bay Crab and Shrimp Reuben

COURTESY OF CHEFS DON AND KATE APPLEBAUM, CAJUN KATE'S

While this dish is nothing like crab imperial, the combination of seafood salad topped with an additional sauce has a similar, rich, effect. And honestly—crab imperial is pretty perfect already, so why mess with a good thing?

Make sure to read this recipe through before starting, as it needs an extra day of prep time to marinate the crab meat. And yes, each sandwich is meant to have a hefty pound of salad. (SERVES 6)

For seafood:

1 onion, roughly chopped

1 cup celery, roughly chopped

1 tablespoon garlic, chopped

⅛ cup celery salt

3 bay leaves

½ cup crab boil seasoning

1 gallon water

½ lemon

2 pounds (21/25 count) shrimp

4 pounds lump crabmeat, picked over for shells

For tartar sauce:

2½ cups mayonnaise

⅓ cup minced onion

⅓ cup minced dill pickles

⅓ cup whole grain mustard

1 tablespoon apple cider vinegar

1 tablespoon pickle juice

½ teaspoon sugar

1 teaspoon crab boil seasoning

Salt and pepper to taste

For crab and shrimp salad:

1½ cups finely diced celery

¾ cups finely diced onion

3 tablespoons lemon juice

1 teaspoon celery salt

Salt and pepper to taste

For coleslaw:

2–2½ cups finely shredded green cabbage

½ cup shredded carrot

¼ cup finely sliced onion

1 ounce apple cider vinegar

½ ounce vegetable oil

1½ teaspoons sugar

1 teaspoon dry mustard

½ cup mayonnaise

Salt and pepper to taste

For Russian dressing:

1 cup mayonnaise

¼ cup ketchup

½ cup relish

Salt and pepper

To assemble:

12 thick cut slices good Jewish rye

12 slices Swiss cheese

Butter for cooking

To cook shrimp: Combine all ingredients except shrimp in a pot, bring to a boil and simmer for 15 minutes. Add the shrimp and cook until they float, about 5 minutes. Cool, peel shells (if you purchased shrimp still in the shell) and chop. Refrigerate until ready to use.

Strain the boiling liquid and place in a container with a lid. Refrigerate until cold. When cold, add the crabmeat and refrigerate overnight. Before using, drain the crabmeat well and discard the liquid.

To make tartar sauce: Combine all ingredients, seasoning with salt and pepper to taste. Refrigerate until ready to use.

To make crab and shrimp salad: Mix all ingredients together with 2½ cups of the tartar sauce. Add the cooked shrimp and the drained crab meat. Adjust flavors as needed with more lemon juice, salt, and pepper.

To make cole slaw: Place vegetables in a large bowl. Whisk together the remaining ingredients, seasoning to taste with salt and pepper. Combine dressing and vegetables, adding additional seasoning, if needed.

To make Russian dressing: Combine all ingredients, seasoning with salt and pepper to taste.

To assemble sandwiches: Place six slices of rye bread on a sheet tray. Spread Russian dressing on each, then layer with a slice of cheese, crab and shrimp salad, cole slaw, and a second slice of cheese. Top with remaining bread slices.

In a large non-stick saute pan over medium heat, melt two teaspoons of butter. Add two sandwiches and cook until bread is golden brown on the bottom. Carefully flip sandwiches and brown the other side, adding more butter as needed. Repeat with remaining sandwiches.

Cut sandwiches in half and serve with your favorite sides.

Crab Dip

While some people may think that crab dip is a recent invention created to satisfy the drunken urges of bar patrons, it's actually been around for quite a long time. Hot dishes comprising crab cooked in a creamy sauce of wine, eggs, and butter and served with toast have been found in cookbooks dating back to the mid-eighteenth-century. In the 1950s, cold crab dip became popular. Today, hot and cold crab dips are likely to contain cream cheese, which serves as both a creamy element and a thickener. Sometimes hot crab dip is used as a topping, as in some versions of chicken Chesapeake and a recent invention called the crab pretzel.

Cold Crab Dip

This dip, adapted from a recipe often made by our friend Wanda Cogan, is always the most popular at any party. At least among those of us who can eat shellfish.
(SERVES 8 SENSIBLE PEOPLE, BUT IT'S PROBABLY BEST TO DOUBLE THE RECIPE)

1 (8-ounce) package cream cheese, softened

2 tablespoons unsalted butter, softened

2 tablespoons full-fat plain Greek yogurt

1 bunch scallions, chopped

Salt and black pepper to taste

6 ounces crab meat, picked over for shells (claw meat works well in this dish)

½ cup cocktail sauce

1 tablespoon prepared horseradish

1 teaspoon freshly squeezed lemon juice

Crackers and crudité for serving

Stir together the cream cheese, butter, and yogurt until completely combined. Add the scallions and season with salt and pepper. Fold in the crabmeat and spread into a shallow bowl.

Combine the cocktail sauce, horseradish, and lemon juice in another bowl. Pour evenly over the cream cheese and crab mixture. Chill until ready to serve.

Crab Pretzel

A crab pretzel is usually a big soft pretzel, the kind with a chewy interior and crisp exterior like those found on New York City street carts, coated with hot crab dip. They are dense and rather messy and best shared with a friend or two. These pretzels are more like the addictive butter-coated ones found in most shopping malls these days, soft and pillowy, and they're served with a delicate dipping sauce made with beer, cheese, and crab. It's still finger food, but infinitely more elegant than the original.

If you plan on feeding this to the kids, near beer can be substituted for the real thing. (SERVES 6–10)

For pretzels:

1 tablespoon active dry yeast

¼ cup light brown sugar

4 cups all-purpose flour

Olive oil

¼ cup baking soda

Flaky sea salt, like Maldon

4 tablespoons unsalted butter, melted

© Kathy Wielech Patterson

For crab fondue:

2 tablespoons unsalted butter

2 tablespoons all-purpose flour

1 cup neutral lager- or pilsner-style beer (like Stella Artois or Corona)

½ cup whole milk

5 ounces Monterey Jack cheese, grated

1 teaspoon Old Bay® Seasoning, or more to taste

¼ teaspoon ground white pepper

Pinch cayenne

Salt to taste

4 ounces of crab meat, preferably body meat or claw, picked over for shells

Finely chopped chives

To make pretzels: Place the yeast, sugar, and 1¼ cups warm (approximately 100°F) water in the bowl of a stand mixer fitted with the dough hook attachment. Allow to sit for 5 minutes or until the mixture begins to foam. Add the flour all at once and mix on low speed until the dough just comes together and pulls away from the side of the bowl, 2 to 3 minutes. Do not overmix or knead or the dough will become tough.

Remove the dough from the bowl and gently form into a ball. Drizzle some olive oil into the bowl and roll the dough ball in it to coat. Place the dough into the bowl, cover with a towel, and set in a warm draft-free place to rise until doubled in size, about an hour.

Once the dough has risen, combine the baking soda and 1½ cups hot water in a bowl.

Preheat oven to 450°F. Prepare two baking sheets by covering them with parchment or silicone baking mats.

Take a portion of the dough and pat into a rectangle about 4 x 4½ inches thick. Trim the sides and cut the rectangle into 4 strips about 4 inches long and 1 inch wide. Dip each strip into the baking soda water and place onto one of the baking sheets. Repeat until all dough is used, including the scraps. Sprinkle tops with sea salt.

Bake pretzels for about 6 minutes, until golden brown. While pretzels are still hot, brush tops with melted butter.

To make fondue: Melt the butter in a saucepan over medium heat. Make a roux by whisking in the flour until completely combined. Cook for 2 minutes, whisking constantly. Gradually pour in the beer and then the milk, whisking the whole time. Once the liquids are incorporated, turn the heat to high and bring to a boil. Reduce the heat to a simmer, then stir in the cheese and the seasonings.

Once the cheese is completely melted, stir in the crab and remove from the heat. Pour into ramekins, garnish with chives and additional Old Bay® Seasoning. Serve immediately with warm soft pretzels for dipping.

One Fish, Two Fish, Rockfish, Bluefish

As the saying goes, "Give a man a fish and you feed him for a day; teach a man to fish and you feed him for a lifetime." That is true only insofar as the fish last.

The Chesapeake Bay was once teeming with fish large and small, from shad and croakers to anchovies and minnows. Some of the more than three hundred species of fish found in the Bay and its tributaries are merely fish food, a source of nutrients for larger creatures in the waterway. Others have served as sustenance for those voracious creatures at the top of the food chain—humans.

Long before Europeans settled the shores of the Chesapeake, Native Americans were enjoying the Bay's bounty. They made camp along waterways and fished using nets and weirs, v-shaped stone obstructions set up to trap or redirect fish. Spears and hooks were also used to catch fish, which the Native Americans smoked over open fires in order to preserve them for later use. Then, the fish were plentiful, and there were far fewer consumers. Once the early settlers arrived, the amount of fish caught not only for sustenance but also sport, increased. It was their right, after all, as granted by Charles I in the Maryland Charter of 1632. It guaranteed: "Fishings of all sortes of Fishe, Whales, Sturgions, and other lioyall Fishes in the Sea or Rivers; and . . . free liberty of Fishing as well in the Sea as in the Ports and Creekes of the Province aforesayed."

The most common method of fishing involved a simple hook and line, with which colonists were able to catch black and red drum, perch, catfish, sheepshead, rockfish, and sturgeon. Later, weirs and seines—large fishing nets with weights at the bottom and floats at the top—were employed. In the late 1800s, with tobacco farming losing its footing as the main moneymaking pursuit of southern Maryland, fishing became an economic mainstay. Over the years, as fish harvests grew, early conservationists went into action. In 1760, the Maryland General Assembly passed a bill to "prevent any making or repairing of any fish dams and pots on the River Susquehanna," and in 1768, weir use was banned on the Susquehanna, Potomac, and Patuxent Rivers. These were among the first Maryland laws for the conservation of its natural resources. Other laws over the years regulated size limits, seasons, and the type of gear used, but nothing really stopped the steady decline of the numbers of fish in the Bay. However, there is still plenty of sport and commercial fishing going on in the Chesapeake. Fish needs to stop being so tasty.

Sounds from Below*

We're going to jump right in and talk about what is probably Baltimore's favorite fish, the lake trout. Sorry to disappoint you, but there's no such thing. Or, rather, there is, but it's not the same fish that is so popular in Maryland's largest city. What we refer to as "lake trout" is neither trout nor from a lake—it's actually any one of about six species of trash fish that are shaped rather like a flattened eel. Most folks will tell you it's "whiting," which may be true, but that doesn't necessarily clarify things. The National Oceanic and Atmospheric Administration (NOAA) says whiting is a name given to various fish from the genus *Merluccius*. Silver hake is probably the best known type of whiting. But don't confuse it with the hake one might find in a better seafood restaurant. Also sometimes called "steakfish," (as is most fish cut crosswise into steaks, rather than lengthwise into fillets), hake is very moist with large flakes and is related to cod and haddock. It's a much larger fish than lake trout. Also don't confuse it with the whiting sold down in the Carolinas, which is actually another name for sea mullet, a member of the mackerel family. Which is not lake trout.

In any case, lake trout doesn't come out of the Chesapeake. It's fished off the Atlantic coast and usually immediately frozen. One would be hard-pressed to say exactly what species of fish any particular specimen called "lake trout" actually is. Still, people like it just the same, battered and fried until crisp, and served between slices of white bread, maybe with ketchup or hot sauce or horseradish. In many cases there are more bones and batter than actual fish, but that doesn't seem to bother lake trout aficionados.

*Title from a song by the Baltimore band Lake Trout.

We Will Rock You

There are rockfish, and there are rockfish. The name is given to several species of fish found in different parts of the world, but here in Maryland, rockfish only means one thing: *Morone saxatilis*, or striped bass. Because of the nomenclatural confusion (of this and other species), the FDA has set a list of acceptable market names. So while it's perfectly fine for Marylanders to call *M. saxatilis* "rockfish," a fish caught in Maryland but sold across state lines must be called "bass." Them's the rules, folks.

The state of Maryland is so fond of this particular sea creature that they made it the state fish in 1965. Sometimes you'll hear rockfish called

"stripers," but mostly not. These delicious creatures are anadromous, spawning in freshwater but spending their adult lives in saltwater, making the brackish waters of the Chesapeake a perfect habitat. So perfect that the populations of striped bass noticeably increase in New England and Mid-Atlantic fisheries in the year following a particularly successful spawning season in the Chesapeake.

These carnivores can reach lengths up to sixty inches and weigh close to seventy pounds. The largest caught in the Chesapeake was just under sixty-eight pounds. A big fish, sure, but the record for the largest caught ever—this one off the coast of North Carolina—is a whopping 125 pounds. In 1891. Yes, over 120 years ago. So not really likely to happen anytime soon. Because the rockfish is such a popular sport fish, it's found not only in the Chesapeake and its tributaries, but also in various landlocked reservoirs like Piney Run and Tridelphia, where it has been stocked for fishing purposes.

Despite a history of overfishing, the Bay's rockfish population is more or less at a sustainable level, thanks to a years-long multi-state fishing moratorium put in place in the late 1980s. We say "more or less," because the

Chesapeake's balance is so delicate, and it really doesn't take a lot to send something that's going well into the opposite direction. Striped bass are predatory carnivores, and there's always the worry that there might not be enough prey available to sustain the currently high levels of these fish in the Bay. Especially with the recent unwanted introduction of various invasive species that also like to dine on the Bay's population of smaller fish like menhaden, shad, and perch.

Then there's a bacterial infection called mycobacteriosis that affects some rockfish. First diagnosed in Bay rockfish in 1997, mycobacteriosis causes a variety of symptoms including skin lesions and stunted growth. It's not known how many fish die from this disease, or if any that do get it recover from it, but both rates are being studied. Currently, the Maryland Department of Natural Resources thinks that as many as 60 percent of Chesapeake rockfish have this disease. In fact, *Mycobacterium marinum* is pretty ubiquitous, estimated to be found in 67 percent of water specimens collected worldwide in over 160 species of fish. However, there's little evidence that Chesapeake fish other than rockfish are affected. We know what you're thinking, "Can humans get mycobacteriosis?" Yes indeed, it is zoonotic, which means the bacterium can make the leap from animals to humans. Once it does, it's usually referred to as "fish handler's disease," and it can be treated with antibiotics. To avoid contracting mycobacteriosis, it's recommended to wear heavy cotton or leather gloves when handling rockfish; boots, too, to avoid being poked in the foot by a fish spine. But if you're not a commercial fisherman or aquaculture worker, the chances of your being infected are slim to none. Another spot of good news—there's no evidence of human-to-human transfer.

As far as anyone can tell, humans won't get sick from eating properly prepared rockfish. It's a common sense thing—if the fish you've caught has lesions on the skin and signs of darkened flesh or hemorrhage inside, then toss it. If it looks sick, it probably is, so don't eat it. To be on the safe side, don't eat rockfish raw (although we know someone who does it, but he's eaten highly poisonous Japanese fugu, too).

Rockfish is at its most delicious cooked, anyway, and wild, if you can get it. Despite the healthy numbers of fish in the Chesapeake, there is a good deal of aquacultured rockfish on the market. And, call us snobs, but we prefer the flavor of wild fish, so that's what we recommend for the dishes included in this chapter.

Bluefish

Pomatomus saltatrix sounds like the name of a character from either Dr. Seuss or Harry Potter (or their lovechild), but most of us just call it bluefish. These long-bodied fish with forked tails and short fins look a lot like children's drawings of fish. But don't let that fool you—the bluefish is a voracious predator. The kind of fish that will kill another fish just for looking at it funny. It mostly uses its sharp teeth to attack prey like squid, menhaden, and anchovies. They'll bite you, too, if you get too close. And they travel in large schools, so it's best not to dangle your hand over the edge of the boat if you know there are bluefish in the area. They're not called "marine

Jay Fleming

Can Community Supported Fisheries (CSFs) Help the Chesapeake Bay?

In recent years, the notion of farmers selling directly to restaurants and individual consumers has turned into a productive direct marketing model for many small businesses. Community Supported Agriculture (CSA) allows consumers to pre-pay for weekly or bi-weekly boxes of produce provided by local farmers directly. Not only is the produce fresher, the arrangement allows farmers to showcase the finest fruits and vegetables that can be grown in their community. The consumers, in turn, have the opportunity to try out food that they might not normally find at the supermarket.

"Farm to table" has become such a hit around the country that many fishermen are trying out a similar model known as "boat to fork." A community supported fishery (CSF) links fishermen with the local market. Participants can pay for a season ticket, as it were, of locally caught seafood delivered on a weekly or bi-weekly basis, just like a CSA. Some CSFs also sell through farmers markets or through dock pick-ups, although health requirements limit this arrangement to whole fish. In some areas, CSFs have established programs with local school systems to provide seafood for their lunch programs. Not only do the children benefit from fresh, nutritional food, they are educated on where their lunch comes from and how it is caught.

This new direct market approach is not simply a foodie trend but rather a way to address some harsh realities for watermen. With declining market prices, depleted stocks, and rising operating costs, fishermen are looking for a way to create a direct link with consumers and increase their share of the profits. Evidence shows that the plan is working. Over a two-year period, Walking Fish CSF in North Carolina earned 33 percent more revenue for their catch over the average monthly ex-vessel price (post-season adjusted price for first purchase of a commercial harvest). Also, Walking Fish made an additional 14 to 18 percent more per dollar using a year-end profit sharing arrangement. Beyond the financial benefits, CSFs increase the bond between fishermen and consumers, thus allowing them greater control in responding to market forces. Greater awareness builds better cooperation and receptivity in addressing the social and ecological issues of their community.

In terms of how CSFs can positively impact the environment, the jury is still out. It's certainly true that CSFs can greatly reduce the carbon footprint of getting the seafood to market when compared to industrial fishing. However, it doesn't really affect the sustainability of certain species that are already in danger. What CSFs can do is encourage fishermen to introduce the consumers to seafood that may be locally abundant, but are not normally offered by industrial fishing operations. Also, fishermen may have greater focus on the local food systems and adopt gear that has less impact on the environment.

CSFs have functioned successfully for many years on the west coast and New England, but are a relatively new idea for the Mid-Atlantic states. Recently, the Oyster Recovery Partnership (ORP) in Maryland started its own CSF called Old Line Fish Company. According to ORP's Paul Schurick, the idea for a CSF grew out of their aquaculture efforts where they train watermen to raise oysters much like farm-raised fish. Although aquaculture can produce a superior product, traditional distribution systems don't always appreciate that when determining price. Since most watermen are more focused on cultivating their product rather than marketing, they may not be able to sell their harvest at the price they would like to receive. Old Line Fish Company sells directly to the public at a price both the watermen and the consumer can live with.

Of course, Old Line Fish Company is not just about oysters. Participants in the program receive a box every two weeks filled with whatever seafood is readily available at that time. Some boxes may contain a pound of crab meat, others may have catfish, and still others may have oysters. The CSF can also focus on invasive species like snakeheads and blue catfish, which need to be culled from the Bay population but have not yet found a market locally.

Old Line Fish Company launched a pilot program in the fall of 2015 with a limited number of subscribers in Annapolis and Easton. As of this writing, the CSF is about to be opened to the public. Although the endeavor is relatively small at this point, Schurick said, "It's a whole new ball game for distribution and marketing."

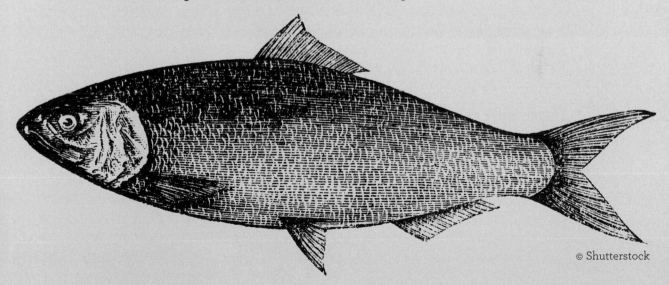

© Shutterstock

piranha" for nothing, so make sure that you're in a position to get your revenge by eating it.

Bluefish aren't particularly large in size, not anymore, but they have the potential to get as big as forty inches. The Chesapeake Bay record is only twenty-five inches, for a fish caught in Virginia; most bluefish average about a foot in length. *P. saltatrix* is a migratory fish, swimming south in the cooler months, so the best time to catch them in the Chesapeake and Mid-Atlantic coast is between April and July, and then again in October and November, after which they head down to warmer climes.

Bluefish are found up and down the Atlantic seaboard, so fishing quotas are set by the federal government rather than individual states. They change every year. In 2014, for example, recreational fishermen—who make up the majority of the fishery—were allowed to catch up to 13.5 million pounds. The commercial quota was a bit over half that amount, 7.4 million. And while in Maryland we tend to think of bluefish as one of our very own, our share of the commercial fishery pot is a wee 3 percent, or just under 224,000 pounds of fish. That's not an insignificant amount of fish, yet it doesn't pop up on restaurant menus all that much these days. A shame, because it's quite delicious.

Because bluefish are predatory, their digestive enzymes are quite strong and will cause rapid spoilage if they aren't broken down and bled shortly after being caught. Some will say that bluefish is "fishy-tasting." (Well, it is *a fish*. Why bother eating fish at all if you don't expect it to taste like fish?) Certainly, they are not bland. They are delicious simply grilled and served with lemon, and their lightly oily flesh really takes to hot-smoking.

Fishin' and Hopin'

As mentioned earlier, there are over 300 species of fish found in the Chesapeake. Some of the smaller fish, like menhaden and anchovies, end up as food for larger fish like perch, bluefish, and rockfish, which end up as food for humans. But there are plenty of other fish in the sea, so to speak, that we don't tend to see on restaurant menus, at least not as often as blue and rock. Some, like blueback herring, have been fished to near extinction; there's been a fishing moratorium on them since December of 2011. The Chesapeake's Atlantic sturgeon is on the Federal Endangered Species List. There's only one spawning population currently known, in the James River in Virginia. There is historical evidence that once there were spawning populations in Maryland in the Potomac and Susquehanna, but that is definitely no longer true. I hate to break it to you, but your great money-making scheme of selling Chesapeake-raised caviar just isn't going to fly.

Menhaden, *Brevoortia tyrannus,* are one of the most important fish in the Bay. While historically they served as crop fertilizer, these tiny fish have a far more important function as a food source for larger predatory fish like rock and blue. Additionally, menhaden are filter feeders, like oysters, so they perform a service for the Bay at large by eating algae and keeping the waters clean. They are also commercially fished as a source of Omega-3-rich fish oil for use in vitamin supplements and cosmetics, and as a popular bait for the Chesapeake's blue crab fishery.

Menhaden travel in huge schools, which makes them pretty easy to catch by purse seine (a giant net of sorts). As with pretty much everything Chesapeake-related, there are those folks who think that the menhaden fishery should be regulated, and those who believe there are more out there than meet the eye. Are there enough to sustain the Bay's rockfish population? That's a concern of recreational fishermen, who rely on striped bass for their sport. Are there enough for the crabbers baiting needs? How about the commercial fishermen, who get the bulk of the harvest each year?

A catch cap has been instituted, but the numbers are still being juggled. Hopefully the fish will win.

Sharks visit the Chesapeake from time to time in the summer and fall. Bull sharks have been seen as far north as the Patuxent River. Sandbar sharks prefer saltier waters and if they come into the Chesapeake, they'd rather hang out in Virginia, as do Sand Tiger sharks. Smaller sharks like the smooth or spiny dogfish also come up the Chesapeake between late fall and early spring, and rarely one will spot a basking or smooth hammerhead shark. All of these guys are just visitors and prefer the saltier waters of the Atlantic Ocean for most of the year. But if you can get your hands on a dogfish (um, carefully though), they do make good eating. It's a meaty, white-fleshed fish that makes delicious fish and chips. However, it's important that people not go crazy and start killing all of the sharks, as they are an important part of the Chesapeake Bay ecosystem. Without them, other fish like the cownose ray, upon which some species of shark feed, tend to over-populate and cause problems. Rays like to eat oysters, for example. And cownose rays are not particularly edible; don't confuse them with skate. These guys urinate through their skin, so their flesh tends to taste like uric acid. They also have a poisonous spine at the base of their tails that makes them less than safe to handle.

Other imminently edible fish that are prevalent in the Chesapeake and its tributaries are croaker, white perch, black drum, trout, and summer and winter flounders. There are also largemouth bass, eel, and mackerel. Snakeheads and blue and flathead catfish are found in the area as well, though they are not indigenous. These invasive species, though harmful to the ecosystem, are tasty and will be discussed in a later chapter.

Thanks for the Memories

Two more denizens of the Chesapeake that have fed the masses over the generations are shad and terrapin. Both have been historically important to the diet of Chesapeake-area residents and deserve their own sections. Unfortunately, they are also two of the most over-fished species in the Bay and while these fisheries have been closed for many years now, the populations are still a long way off from making a comeback.

Shad Songs (Say So Much)

There is a popular story that maintains shad saved George Washington's Continental Army from famine after the particularly hard winter of 1778. The legend says that an early spring shad run came up the Schuylkill River that ran near the Valley Forge camp allowing soldiers to catch thousands of the fat fish, eat their fill, then salt and preserve barrels of more fish for later consumption.

Like rockfish, shad are anadromous; while they spend much of their lives in saltwater, they swim to freshwater to spawn. Apparently, the enemy British knew this factoid and blocked the shad's path up the Schuylkill, so they never made it to Valley Forge. Indeed, archaeologists have revealed that while cattle and pig bones were found at the Valley Forge camp site, there were no fish bones. Great story though. What is true is that George Washington was a commercial shad fisherman. The Potomac River ran along the boundary of his Mount Vernon estate, and he was able to catch some of the millions of shad on their way upstream to spawn. He sold much of the fish, but some he kept for his slaves. The rest, he salted and kept year-round as rations. It's possible that it was some of his store of salted fish that accompanied his men to Valley Forge, but that doesn't make for a very dramatic story.

© Jay Fleming

Before Washington's time, shad was an important source of protein for other people in the Chesapeake Bay region. It was a staple food for the North Americans and European settlers both. Yet one doesn't see shad on menus very often these days.

Shad has always been a seasonal fish, primarily eaten in spring, as they were easier to catch on their migration from the Atlantic to freshwater spawning grounds. As the population in the Bay area increased, particularly in the last half of the eighteenth century, when the population nearly tripled, the demand for shad also rose. About 45,000 tons of shad were harvested annually in the 1830s and 1840s, falling to less than 10,000 tons by the end of that century. By the 1970s, the annual catch brought in only about 1,000 tons of shad. Overfishing wasn't the only problem; the creation of dams that blocked the fish's entry to rivers was also an issue. In the 1980s, Maryland closed its fisheries for both American and Hickory shad and began restoration programs, to prevent the species extinction from its waters. Dams have been removed, and the Maryland Department of

© Jay Fleming

Natural Resources has started stocking the Choptank and Patapsco Rivers with juvenile shad and larvae.

The numbers of shad in the Bay have increased in recent years, due to improvements in water quality and the grass beds that form habitat for the fish in addition to the fishing moratorium and restocking efforts.

One of the reasons that shad were so popular, besides being fairly plentiful at one time, is that they are quite tasty fish. Shad are members of the *Clupeidae* family, making them herrings, like the sardine. And like the sardine, they have a rich, fatty, flesh. They also have lots of bones, making them a bit fiddly to prepare, but the flavor is well worth the effort. All a shad fillet needs is a light saute in butter, a squeeze of lemon, and bon appetit! The roe, too, are quite delicious, and a great delicacy with an extremely short season.

Shad roe in the marketplace is a harbinger of spring. The roe come in pairs of ruby red sacs that more resemble something from a land animal than from a fish. They are generally served intact, that is with the sac, as cooking the eggs separately may cause them to become gritty and a bit tough in texture. A nice way to cook shad roe is to dredge them in a bit of seasoned flour and saute them until golden brown on both sides. When they are firm to the touch, they are done. They're especially good for breakfast, topped with crisp bacon and perhaps some caramelized onions. The flavor is lightly metallic, a bit livery, but otherwise mild.

There is a third type of shad in the Chesapeake, the Gizzard shad. There are no restrictions to catching this particular fish—nobody wants them. It's not particularly edible, having soft, tasteless flesh and lots of bones.

Fear the Turtle

The Diamondback terrapin (*Malaclemys terrapin*) is Maryland's official state reptile. The state is so into the whole turtle thing that the University of Maryland named their sports teams after them, although we tend to shorten it to "Terps." The team's mascot, Testudo, is named for the order to which these reptiles belong, Testudines.

While the terrapin is technically not a fish, and currently not quite an endangered species, its harvest has been verboten in Maryland since 2007. Diamondback terrapins, so named because of the pattern of concentric diamond shapes on their backs, had long been harvested for their meat; once they were both cheap and plentiful. Such were their numbers that Chesapeake-area landowners used terrapin as a major source of protein for their servants and slaves. So much terrapin was on the menu that the slaves rebelled, demanding diversity in their diets. Eventually the numbers of turtles declined, and their meat became more of a luxury item. Terrapin soup appeared on the menus of fancy restaurants, and was served at the White House. The once-plentiful product of the Chesapeake that sold for a dollar a wagonload in colonial times soon rose to over $100 a dozen in the mid-1800s. By 1902, the U.S. Bureau of Fisheries (now the U.S. Fish and Wildlife Service) was looking into turtle farming, which they gave up when the fashion for turtle soup waned.

The human gullet hasn't been the only hazard to diamondback terrapins. Raccoons love them, too, as do eagles, gulls, and the occasional shark. The uptick in waterfront housing has led to the disappearance of the beaches so essential to nesting, and the salt marshes that they live in are rapidly disappearing. The crab pots used to catch blue crabs are also a

© Jay Fleming

hazard: terrapins tend to be attracted to the same bait, crawl into a pot, and in many cases, drown.

While the heyday of Turtlemania ended in the 1800s, the occasional recipe for terrapin still appeared in cookbooks all the way into the 1970s, including *The Joy of Cooking*. Many twentieth-century Maryland cookbooks included at least one recipe for terrapin. Perhaps diamondback terrapin is a tasty morsel, but preparation seemed a tricky proposition, requiring both time and labor. Most recipes caution cooks to not break the gall bladder. Some call for the turtle to be bled before cooking, others advise cooking them live. There was also boiling or soaking, shell and toenail removal, entrail sorting, and meat chopping involved, and this was just the prep work. Cooking terrapin made a crab feast seem like child's play.

Perhaps it was the work involved or the expense of the ingredient or a combination of the two that prompted many a cook to resort to rustling up a pot of mock terrapin, instead. There doesn't seem to be a set recipe for creating a dish of faux turtle, nor is there a standard protein substitute. There are mock terrapin recipes that call for beef liver, calf's head (with brains) or feet, various cooked poultry items including chicken, turkey, and duck, and veal or beef. It's said that the meat from different parts of the turtle are similar to these sundry proteins, which would explain the recipe calling for calf's head, and veal, and poultry . . . and ham. Some of the mock turtle recipes also involve hard-boiled eggs, and/or meatballs, which presumably would stand in for turtle eggs.

Eventually, the words "mock turtle," were used most frequently with the word "soup." Even Campbell's offered a version, said to be a favorite of the artist Andy Warhol.

Clam Bam, No Thank You Ma'am

Speaking of not technically a fish, there are clams in the Chesapeake, although the Bay's not particularly famous for them. For some reason, eating clams was never popular in these parts, not like it is in, say, New England. There's no famous recipe for Maryland Clam Chowder, and the

Clam terminology

Restaurants that serve hard shell clams might use terms like "quahogs," "littlenecks," or "cherrystones," on their menus. One might think they refer to different types of clams, or perhaps to where they were harvested, but the names are actually assigned to the size of the clam. All of them are quahogs (co-hogs), or *Mercenaria mercenaria*. Littlenecks are the smallest quahogs, measuring about 1½ to 2 inches across; cherrystones are 2 to 2½ inches; and chowder clams are about 4 inches in diameter. They tend to be chewy, so they work best in dishes like chowders where they can be simmered for a good long time.

mention of fried clams around these parts usually conjures up either Mrs. Paul's or, ah, Friendly's. Sad, but true.

There are both hard clams and soft clams in the Chesapeake, although not all that many of the former. The latter are usually referred to as "maninose," and, for no good reason in particular, are largely scorned by Marylanders. That is, those few who actually know they exist. *Mya arenaria* (aka belly, Ipswich, or steamer clams) resemble the famous geoduck clams of the Pacific Northwest (to which they are not related) in that they have a leathery neck, or siphon, that sticks out of one end of their shell. If disturbed, they will pull in their siphon and squirt a column of water, earning them the charming sobriquet, "piss clams."

Despite their existence in the Bay since forever, commercial soft clam harvesting didn't start until the early 1950s. And it didn't take long for the population to decline. It wasn't harvesting alone that hurt the Bay's clams, however. The population in the Virginia end of the Bay was affected by disease, ending the fishery there before 1970. Maryland had a disease-related catastrophe in 1971, then hurricane Agnes did a number on the remaining population in 1972. Other factors affected the soft shell clam population after Agnes, and today, harvesters are limited to between eight and fifteen bushels per day, depending on the season. And it's a real shame that there aren't more maninose in the Bay. Like oysters, they are filter feeders, which mean they can help keep the waters clean. They're also a big ol' lump of easy-to-reach protein for predators like blue crabs, eels, and the currently problematic cownose rays that have been feeding on oysters instead. Waterfowl and raccoons love them, too. As do New Englanders (and a handful of Marylanders), who like to eat them fried.

There are delicious razor clams in the Bay, too, but they are primarily harvested for use as crab bait.

Go Fish

There are, of course, many species of fish in the Bay that are not particularly edible, at least not by our standards. There are seahorses, and pipefish (which are like seahorses but long and skinny), and their cousins, the sticklebacks. Other small fish, like gobies and blennies, hogchokers, and tessellated darters live in the Bay, too. All serve a purpose, whether it's to eat mosquitos or to serve as food for larger fish or aquatic birds. Were we all so useful.

Bill Burton

Most Marylanders of a certain age remember Bill Burton. Many of us can still picture his black beard boldly streaked with white, as seen in the still image of his visage that accompanied his tinny-sounding pre-recorded fisheries reports on WMAR-TV.

Originally from Providence, Rhode Island, Burton served in the Navy Seabees as an underwater demolition expert during World War II. Once home from the war, Burton attended Goddard College in Vermont on the G.I. bill, where he majored in journalism. During his junior year, he worked for a radio station in Montpelier, but soon switched to newspapers. In 1956, the *Baltimore Sun* hired him as a full-time outdoors reporter, a position he held for thirty-seven years. He also wrote for the *Annapolis Capital* and the *Bay Weekly*, edited several regional hunting and fishing magazines, and was one of the three founding members of the Mason-Dixon Outdoors Writers Association. Burton taught both fishing and journalism at Anne Arundel Community College and Chesapeake College. And in 2009, he was inducted into the MD-DE-DC Press Association Hall of Fame. He was even named an "Admiral of the Chesapeake" by Maryland Governor J. Millard Tawes. He fished with Presidents Eisenhower and George H.W. Bush, with local politicians like Senator Barbara Mikulski, and Governors Mandel, Tawes, and McKeldin, and sports stars like Johnny Unitas, Boog Powell, and Ted Williams. He even cast a line with fellow writer Ernest Hemingway.

During his time with the *Sun*, Burton's writing focused on the Chesapeake, and he saw many patterns of decline and resurgence among the Bay's fauna. He loved eating white perch, rockfish, and smoked bluefish, and especially shad and shad roe, and hoped to live long enough to see shad fishery come back to the Bay.

Bill Burton died on August 10, 2009, at the age of eighty-two. Shad fishery is still verboten. But while he wasn't able to see that creature's resurgence, he's lending his name to an effort to restore some habitat to the Bay.

In the 1980s, when the new four-lane Senator Frederick C. Malkus, Jr., Memorial Bridge was being erected over the Choptank River in Cambridge, Maryland, Burton lobbied for the old bridge to be saved and used as a fishing pier. It was, and just prior to his death, the old bridge was named in his honor.

In 2013, an artificial oyster reef was constructed alongside the Bill Burton Fishing Pier. Built by the Chesapeake Bay Foundation (CBF), the Maryland Artificial Reef Initiative (MARI), and the Maryland Department of Natural Resources, the reef consists of three hundred submerged concrete "reef balls" on which creatures like oysters, barnacles, and mussels can attach themselves. The reef also serves as a habitat for fish like croaker and rockfish, and for crustaceans like blue crabs. The Bill Burton reef is one of the most accessible such reefs on the Eastern Shore, and a great place to cast a line.

Smoked Bluefish Rillettes with Citrus and Herb Salad

COURTESY OF CHEF ZACK MILLS, WIT & WISDOM

Like mackerel, salmon, and other oily fish, bluefish takes really well to smoking. If you can find it at a local smoked fish purveyor (like Neopol Savory Smokery in Baltimore's Belvedere Square Market), then most of the work has been done for you. If you prefer to smoke your own fish, then you can use the recipe following this one. Plating this dish requires a ring mold. If you don't have one handy, you can use a standard tuna can with the top and bottom cut off. Washed thoroughly, of course. Or, you can just rough it by forming a small mound of the rillettes and flattening it out to a circle with the back of a spoon. (SERVES 8)

For rillettes:

1 pound smoked bluefish

⅛ cup canola oil

½ cup diced fennel

¼ cup diced celery

2 shallots, minced

1 clove garlic, minced

2 tablespoons chopped fresh tarragon

2 tablespoons chopped fresh parsley

2 tablespoons minced chives

¼ teaspoon Old Bay® Seasoning

3 tablespoons crème fraiche

Juice of 1 lemon

2 tablespoons prepared horseradish

For salad:

2 cups frisée

¼ cup parsley leaves

¼ cup tarragon leaves

¼ cup mint leaves

1 orange, cut into segments

⅛ cup extra virgin olive oil

Salt to taste

To serve:

1 baguette, cut into thin slices

⅛ cup extra virgin olive oil

1 tablespoon salt

1 teaspoon black pepper

To make rillettes: Break bluefish up into approximately 1-inch pieces. Set aside.

In a saute pan over medium heat, add canola oil. Cook fennel, celery, shallots, and garlic, stirring occasionally, until translucent, about 3 minutes. Remove from the heat and add the chopped herbs and Old Bay® Seasoning.

ack Mills

Using a stand mixer with a paddle attachment, combine bluefish, cooked vegetables and herbs, crème fraiche, lemon juice, and horseradish. Mix on low speed until mixture becomes homogenous. Scoop rillettes into a covered container and refrigerate until ready to use.

To make salad: Combine frisée and herbs in a bowl. Cut orange segments in half width-wise and add to salad. Dress gently with olive oil and season with salt.

To serve: Preheat oven to 350°F. Place baguette slices in a single layer on a baking sheet. Drizzle with olive oil and salt and pepper. Bake for about 8 minutes until well toasted. Remove from oven and set aside.

Place a 3- or 4-inch ring mold in the center of a plate. Scoop about 2 ounces of the rillettes mixture into the mold and press down evenly. Gently remove the mold and place a handful of salad on top of the rillettes. Serve with baguette slices.

The Mind of a Fisherman

From time immemorial, man has fished to provide sustenance. But not everyone who goes out with rod and reel hopes to bring dinner back to the homestead. Many recreational fishermen do it for an entirely different reason. Chad Wells lives for fishing. He will even admit that it is an addiction for him. We asked him why exactly he loved the sport, and after he finished explaining it to us, it made lots of sense.

"The main reason I fish is . . . serenity.

"The most successful days fishing are ones where you find this balance. You're casting over and over again in the perfect cadence. From making the same motion over and over again, you find this confidence. You don't know when a fish is going to take your bait, or if a fish is going to take your bait, but when it does, it's amazing. You go from peaceful and serene to bang! There it is. There's a split second to make the right decision, get the fish on the boat, and in most cases put the fish back in the water. Sometimes you start thinking about [this fishing trip] days before or even weeks before. Putting your plan together. And then in a millisecond, it happens and you have a feeling of everything paying off.

"The first fish of the day is the best, even if it's a baby. Because you know what you're doing is working."

But even a bad day on the water isn't truly bad, "If you don't catch anything, you can go back and reassess your plan and think about what you did wrong and what you can do differently next time. You get time to think about all of the different variables."

When asked if he was trying to fool nature, Wells said, "Not trying to outsmart the fish but entice it to do something. You're trying to mimic nature. I use artificial lures, some of which I make. It keeps me occupied with fishing when fishing season is over. But you can't predict nature 100 percent; you can have a day when you're out on the water and it's not what you expected. The water is brown, the grass bed is dead, and you have to employ plan b or plan c.

"There are three Cs of fishing: colors, conditions, and confidence. You can almost throw color out the window. Some people can be successful using the same color bait all year long, and they catch fish because of their confidence. I have confidence baits too, that I use when my original plan doesn't work."

"Once your confidence is there, you'll start catching fish."

Smoked Bluefish

¾ cup kosher salt

½ cup sugar

2 pounds bluefish fillets

Vegetable oil

Combine the salt and sugar. Coat the fillets on both sides with the cure mixture. Place fillets on a metal rack set over a sheet tray and refrigerate, uncovered, for about 12 hours.

Rinse the cure from the fish and pat dry. Place the fillets on a clean rack and allow to dry at room temperature for about an hour.

To smoke on a kettle grill: Soak a handful of hardwood chips in water for a few hours. Set up your grill for indirect cooking over very low heat (200°F), according to manufacturer's directions. Drain the wood chips and spread over the coals. Put a drip pan on the cool side. Put the grate on the kettle, cover, and wait until it starts smoking.

Brush fish fillets with a little oil and place on grate over the drip pan. Cook until fish is firm and internal temperature is 140°F, about 45 minutes, depending on the thickness of the fish.

To smoke with a stovetop smoker: Place the smoking chips in the bottom of the smoker. Put on the drip pan and rack. Brush the fish with a little oil and lay it on the rack. Put the lid partway on the smoker and put it on the stovetop. Heat over medium heat until wisps of smoke come out from the pan. Close the lid completely and cook the fish for about 15 minutes.

Refrigerate fish to cool completely before flaking.

Roasted Bluefish with Crab, Corn, and Fennel Salad

COURTESY OF CHEF WINSTON BLICK, CLEMENTINE

Winston says, "This is one of my favorite dishes. The bluefish, crab, and sweet corn were all things we ate regularly growing up around the Bay. Remember, fresh bluefish is a must. Look for filets with no cracks in the meat and the only odor should be of the Bay! Fresh blue is the best eating fish around. We also use crab claw meat because it has a sweet, nutty flavor. Think of it as the dark meat of the crab. This dish is crying to be served with a sweet and vinegary tomato and cucumber salad. I hope you enjoy it."
(SERVES 4–6)

For the fish:

1 lemon

1 small (2–3 pounds) bluefish fillet

Kosher salt

Fresh ground black pepper

1 tablespoon unsalted butter cut into 3 pieces

Several sprigs fresh herbs, such as tarragon, parsley, thyme

For the salad:

1 small fennel bulb

1 pound Maryland crab claw meat, picked over for shell

1½ cups of cooked sweet corn from about 3 cobs

1 small red onion, finely diced

2 tablespoons olive oil

1 whole lemon

1 tablespoon honey

Kosher salt

Fresh cracked black pepper

To make fish: Preheat oven to 400°F. Cut lemon in half. Slice one half into three pieces. Rinse the fish and pat dry. Place it skin-side-down in a non-reactive baking dish. Squeeze the intact lemon half over the fish. Sprinkle with salt and pepper and place the pieces of butter on top. Arrange the herbs on the fish and top with the three slices of lemon. Bake fish for about 20 minutes.

To make salad: Cut the top off the fennel bulb. Slice bulb in half, cut out the core, and slice the rest thinly. Pick out some of the nicer fronds and give them a rough chop. Combine fennel, fronds, crab, corn, and onion in a large bowl. In a smaller bowl, whisk together olive oil, lemon, and honey. Season with the salt and pepper. Toss dressing with vegetables and crab. Add more salt, pepper, and lemon juice to taste.

To serve: Cut bluefish into six 8-ounce portions. Serve each portion with some of the salad.

Sriracha "Bouillabaisse"

We first tasted a version of this dish at the now-closed Baltimore restaurant, Ixia. We enjoyed it so much, we reverse-engineered chef Edward Kim's spicy soup at home. A relatively small amount of effort gives it big flavors. You can use any type of white-fleshed fish that you like in this recipe, including rockfish or other bass, grouper, or cod (which doesn't come from the Chesapeake, but it still works). If you have clams, whether in the shell or canned (we won't tell), add them when you add the fish.
(SERVES 4)

1 tablespoon olive oil

1 medium onion, finely diced

1 clove garlic, minced

2 (15-ounce) cans diced tomatoes

2 (8-ounce) bottles clam juice or 2 cups fish stock

1 tablespoon honey or agave nectar, or to taste

Sriracha chile sauce

Salt and pepper to taste

1 pound white fish fillets, cut into 2-inch pieces

½ pound crab meat, picked over for shells

Chopped parsley or cilantro

French bread

In a Dutch oven or heavy soup pot, heat olive oil and saute onion until translucent. Add the garlic and cook for a minute or 2, stirring frequently so the garlic doesn't burn. Add tomatoes with their juices, clam juice or fish stock and 2 cups of water. Bring to a boil, then reduce to a simmer. Add honey. Cover and let broth simmer for 45 minutes to 1 hour, to allow flavors to meld. Add Sriracha to taste (if you don't like a lot of heat, start with a tablespoon, otherwise add more) and salt and pepper, if needed.

Once the broth's flavor is pleasing to your palate, add the fish directly to the soup and cook only until opaque, about 5 minutes. Stir gently so as not to break it up too much. Add crab just before serving.

Ladle into bowls and sprinkle with parsley or cilantro. Serve with toasted and buttered French bread to mop up the juices.

Maryland Seafood and Stout Chowder

COURTESY OF CHEF ANNMARIE LANGTON, GYPSY QUEEN CAFE

There's not only rockfish in this chowder, but also crab and oysters, the Chesapeake Trifecta. The recipe also calls for Pearl Necklace Oyster Stout, produced by Flying Dog Brewery in Frederick, Maryland. Though located in Western Maryland, Flying Dog understands that we all need to do our part to save our greatest resource. Proceeds from the sale of Pearl Necklace go to the Oyster Restoration Partnership, which coordinates restoration projects in the Chesapeake Bay. If you can't get your hands on Pearl Necklace, Guinness will do just fine.
(SERVES 4–6)

¼ pound applewood smoked bacon, cut into lardons

4 tablespoons unsalted butter

½ cup all-purpose flour

2 cups heavy cream

2 cups whole milk

1 cup clam juice or seafood stock

½ pound rockfish, cut into 1-inch pieces

½ pound crabmeat, picked over for shells

1 pint shucked oysters and their liquor

1 bottle stout, preferably Flying Dog Pearl Necklace Oyster Stout

Old Bay® Seasoning or salt to taste

Maryland beaten biscuits (see recipe on page 144) or oyster crackers, for serving

In a large pot over medium heat, cook the bacon until crisp. Remove bacon from pot and set aside. Turn the heat to low, add the butter to the bacon grease in the pot, and allow to melt. Add the flour and cook for 2 to 3 minutes, stirring constantly to form a thick blond roux.

Pour in the cream and milk, whisking the liquids into the roux to avoid lumps, then add the clam juice. Turn the heat up to medium and add the fish. Cook for about 5 minutes, until fish is opaque. Add the crabmeat and oysters and their liquor and cook for an additional 2 minutes.

Stir in the stout and bring to a simmer. Cook for 8 to 10 minutes, until thickened. Season to taste with Old Bay® Seasoning or salt.

Top with reserved bacon and serve with Maryland beaten biscuits or oyster crackers.

Rockfish with Sweet Potato Hash and Caper Cream

COURTESY OF CHEF CHRIS VOCCI, ALEXANDRA'S TURF VALLEY

This hash is full of textures and flavors: sweet potato, spicy sausage, the crunch of sweet corn. You may be tempted to skip the fish entirely and serve it for breakfast, topped with a couple of poached eggs. We won't tell.
(SERVES 6)

For the hash:

1 cup diced andouille sausage

3 cups diced sweet potatoes with skins on

1 cup diced red onion

1 cup diced red bell pepper

Olive oil, if needed

1 cup (1-inch-long) asparagus pieces

1 cup corn kernels

1 tablespoon blackening seasoning

Salt to taste

For the caper cream:

⅛ cup diced shallots

½ cup diced fennel

½ tablespoon minced garlic

1 tablespoons capers, plus 1 teaspoon brine

1 tablespoon olive oil

¾ cups dry vermouth

1 quart heavy cream

2 sprigs fresh thyme

1 bay leaf

2 tablespoons cornstarch

Salt and pepper to taste

For the rockfish:

6 (7-ounce) skin-on rockfish fillets

Salt and pepper

2 tablespoons olive oil

1 tablespoon unsalted butter

To make hash: Place sausage in a large saute pan over medium heat. Cook until the fat begins to render. Add the sweet potatoes and cook until potatoes start to caramelize and soften, regularly turning them over with a spatula so as not to crush them. Add the onions and peppers and continue to cook until they are soft, turning everything regularly and scraping up any bits that have stuck to the pan. If they start to stick too much, add a bit of olive oil. Add the asparagus, corn, and blackening seasoning and cook only until the asparagus is tender but still retains its color. Check for seasoning and add more salt, if needed. Keep warm until ready to use.

To make the caper cream: In a large saucepot over medium heat, sweat shallots, fennel, garlic, and capers in 1 tablespoon of olive oil, stirring frequently. When vegetables have softened, deglaze the pan with the vermouth. Turn up the heat and bring the mixture to a boil, scraping up any bits that have stuck to the pan.

Reduce liquid by half, then add the heavy cream, thyme, and bay leaf. Simmer over medium heat until mixture has reduced by one quarter.

© Ed Sincavage

Make a slurry with the cornstarch and enough tap water to make a runny paste. Stir as much of it into the sauce to thicken it to your liking.

Strain the sauce, season with salt and pepper to taste. Keep warm until ready to use.

To make the fish: Season fillets with salt and pepper on both sides. Heat two large nonstick pans over medium-high heat. Add olive oil and butter to pans. When butter is melted, add rockfish pieces, one at a time, skin-side down.

Cook for 3 to 4 minutes, pressing down gently with a spatula to ensure crisp skin. Flip pieces and cook an additional 3 to 4 minutes, until cooked through (to an internal temperature of 145°F).

To serve: Make a pile of hash on each of six plates and top with a fish filet, skin-side up. Pour sauce around hash.

Crispy Rockfish Tacos

COURTESY OF CHEF ANNEMARIE LANGTON, GYPSY QUEEN CAFE

This taco recipe is infinitely adjustable according to your whims. The instructions call for deep frying the rockfish, but you can certainly shallow fry the panko-coated fish if you prefer. Or, if you're not into crispy so much, season the fish with salt and smoked paprika and grill it until cooked through. As for the slaw, you can add julienned jicama, fennel, carrot, shredded raw sugar snap peas, whatever you like and have on hand.

The aioli recipe makes a lot. Once you try it though, you'll be happy to slather it on everything from turkey sandwiches to hamburgers.
(SERVES 8–10)

For fish:
1 pound rockfish fillets
1 cup rice flour
1 teaspoon salt
1 teaspoon smoked paprika
3 eggs
1 cup panko
Vegetable oil for frying

For sauce:
2 cups mayonnaise
1 tablespoon minced garlic
1 tablespoon minced chipotle in adobo
1 tablespoon sugar

For slaw:
1 cup shredded green cabbage
1 cup shredded purple cabbage
1 cup chopped cilantro

To serve:
16 taco-sized corn tortillas
1 cup sliced radish
Lime wedges
Sriracha, or your favorite hot sauce
Cilantro

To make fish: Cut the fish into uniform small pieces, 1 x 2-inches or so and set aside.

Sift together flour, salt, and paprika and place on a plate. Beat eggs with ¼ cup water in a bowl. Put the panko on another plate.

In a heavy deep pan or deep fryer, heat six cups of vegetable oil to 375°F.

Roll fish pieces in flour, then coat with egg and then panko. Drop each piece gently into the hot oil and cook until each is golden brown, about 1½ minutes per side. Place cooked fish on paper towel–lined plates to drain.

To make aioli: Combine ingredients in a blender and puree until smooth. Add a few drops of water to thin it out if it seems too thick.

To make slaw: Combine vegetables in a bowl and set aside.

To assemble: Double up the tortillas and toast them in a hot, dry, skillet (or grill them). Add some of the slaw, sliced radishes, and a couple pieces of fish. Drizzle on some of the aioli, a squeeze of lime, hot sauce, and a few sprigs of cilantro. Fold up and eat immediately.

Part 3
Living off the Land

The Chesapeake Bay region is famous not only for its seafood, but also for the various products that come from its shores. A Maryland summer just wouldn't be the same if we couldn't feast on locally grown fruit and vegetables, like corn, tomatoes, and strawberries. Tobacco was the area's biggest cash crop for many generations, but plants like hemp, flax, and rye were also important products, as were naturally occurring resources like black walnut trees. In the last century, chickens became an important source of income for Marylanders, as well as a food source for the entire country. In this chapter, we examine some of Maryland's non-aquatic flora and fauna and their impact on our cuisine.

The Land of Pleasant Living: Farming on the Eastern Shore

While it seemed the earliest aristocratic settlers did not take to farming initially, they soon learned that "he who will not work shall not eat" wasn't just a clever aphorism. Eventually, not only did they grow tobacco for fun and profit, but also nourishing foods to sustain them through the Mid-Atlantic region's sweltering summers and mild winters. This was partly because of legislation requiring that tobacco farmers also plant food crops like corn. Maryland's unique method of farming, a blend of European and Native American techniques devised through trial and error, became known as Chesapeake husbandry.

Both tobacco and corn deplete soil nutrients. Normally, farmers would have manure to use as fertilizer to replenish these nutrients, but there were a couple issues with that. For one thing, using some manures on tobacco—like hog manure—made the tobacco taste bad (as if it tastes good to begin with). Also, in those days, domestic livestock was usually free-range. Without fencing to corral the animals, there weren't handy deposits of manure for the farmers to access. This led to adopting a long-fallow system, which involves growing tobacco for three years, followed by another three of corn. Corn has a deeper root system, so it can draw its nutrients from a different layer of soil. After these six years, however, the land then needs to lie fallow for twenty years before profitable crops can again be grown on it. With this system, a fifty-acre plantation would have only about one-tenth of the land in cultivation at any time. Half the acreage would be woodlands, another quarter pasture, and the remaining land would be fallow.

While tobacco did bring in big money for a while, price fluctuations caused some economic instability in the Maryland colony. Farmers were encouraged to grow hemp and flax and were even subsidized by the local government. And no, it's not what you are thinking—there is no evidence that the colonists were keen on getting high. Nor were they interested in controlling their cholesterol. Hemp fiber is strong, durable, resistant to decay, and makes great rope, thread, cloth, and paper. The same goes for flax, another crop grown to use in textiles. This was especially important to the colonies when relations with the British took a downturn. Rather than continuing to import fabric for use in clothing, hemp was employed. And when war broke out, hemp was indispensable as the source of sails and rope for naval vessels. A heavy frigate (think *U.S.S. Constitution*) could require fifty tons of hemp fiber for its rigging alone.

Frances Burman

After the Revolution, wheat and grains became more popular crops throughout the state, but in Southern Maryland, tobacco remained important and indeed was grown there into the end of the twentieth century. In the early 2000s, Maryland offered a buyout to tobacco growers—ten years of payments equal to the money they would have made with average production, plus the tools they'd need to develop other agricultural businesses or grow alternative crops. Those farmers are now growing vegetables, raising livestock, or have gone into a completely different agricultural direction by growing wine grapes and nursery plants.

The Meat of the Matter

Of course there is more to farming than just hemp and tobacco. One could never accuse Europeans of the seventeenth century of vegetarianism, and it is thought that the very first ships that brought colonists to the New World

© Frances Burman

also brought chickens, pigs, and cows. Cows were raised primarily for their milk, but chickens were useful for both eggs and meat. Pigs, introduced to the mainland by Hernando de Soto in 1539, became the colonists' favorite protein. Within a handful of years, de Soto's original herd of thirteen pigs had grown to many hundred, including those that ran off and became feral pigs. Sir Walter Raleigh introduced pigs to the Mid-Atlantic area when he brought sows to the Jamestown colony in 1607. It wasn't long before pigs were everywhere. While we think of bulls and bears when it comes to Wall Street, the road was actually named for the barriers erected to keep hordes of pigs gone wild out of lower Manhattan. While we're on the topic of Wall Street, the term "pork barrels" refers to actual surplus pork. After pig farmers took supplies of salt pork, bacon, and ham for their own use, they salted and preserved the rest of it in barrels. A man's wealth could be measured in the amount of pork squirreled away for later use.

Speaking of squirrel, Bay-area Marylanders ate those too, along with other wild game large and small—elk, deer, rabbit, duck—all tasty animals.

Then there's muskrat. Many an old-timer on the Eastern Shore will tell you about eating them. These semi-aquatic rodents live in marshy, shallow-water areas, feeding on roots and rhizomes but also the occasional frog or fish. These stinky critters, so named because of the odor adults emit to communicate with one another, have thick, glossy, fur that makes for warm apparel. In the early twentieth century, trapping muskrats for their fur was a popular industry. A 1937 article in the *Journal of Mammalogy* claims that "Maryland muskrats . . . are the largest, darkest, and most valuable of any in the whole world."

The same article also states that, "carefully dressed to avoid a trace of musk, properly cooked and served, their meat is sweet, rich and tender, with the gamy flavor of wild duck." Why, what else would one do with piles of skinned muskrats than to eat them?

While muskrat meat is still eaten by some, available at Baltimore's Lexington Market even today, we've made an executive decision not to include recipes. Our apologies to muskrat lovers the world over.

Against the Grain

Let's go back to tobacco for a moment. Not every farmer in Maryland practiced Chesapeake husbandry. Some farmers had small plots of land and couldn't afford for it to lay idle so they planted a cold-hardy cover crop, like wheat or rye, in the fall. Not only could the grain replenish nutrients in the soil that had been removed by tobacco, it could also protect the fields against wind and water erosion. Rye could be turned into hay for animal feed, or ploughed into the soil to act as a fertilizer. It can also be used to make a tasty adult beverage.

Maryland was once synonymous with rye whiskey. Before the Prohibition, not only was Maryland-style rye popular here, but elsewhere in the country as well. It was likely during the Civil War, with thousands of non-residents coming in and out of Maryland, that the good word about the quality and flavor of our rye whiskey was spread to other states. After the war, new distilleries popped up to meet with the country's demand for rye whiskey. One of these was Orient Distilleries. The owner, Edwin Walters, was the brother of William T. Walters, himself a liquor magnate and art aficionado whose collection later would become Baltimore's world-famous Walters Art Museum. Walters claimed that his distillery was Baltimore's largest; by the 1870s, Orient Pure Rye was available as far away as San Francisco. Another Baltimore-area distillery, Sherwood, was popular enough that by 1878, the Army's Medical Purveying Depot in New York was stockpiling their rye whiskey for hospital use. By the end of the 1800s, at least eight more rye distilleries opened in Baltimore, and dozens more in Western Maryland.

At the turn of the twentieth century, the words "Maryland" and "rye" went together like "Florida" and "orange," or "Georgia" and "peach." Yet within twenty years, the heyday of rye would come to a screeching halt.

Prohibition, certified on January 16, 1919, declared the production, sale, and transportation of alcohol illegal. It didn't take effect until a year later, giving rye aficionados and drunks alike time to sock away a stash of booze before it disappeared. Maryland was the only state that ratified the amendment but refused to enforce it; the governor at the time, Albert C. Ritchie, opposed the amendment as a restriction on Maryland's liberties. Though Maryland refused to play along, Prohibition was the law of the land and soon bootlegging became a popular industry. The Chesapeake Bay became an entryway for illegal hooch, and Maryland was one of the "wettest" states. The city of Baltimore was chock-a-block with speakeasies, and many Maryland residents took to making their own potent potables. There were even neighborhood shops, known as "malt and hops" stores, that sold beer-making supplies under the guise of baking ingredients.

As the years passed, more and more states joined Maryland in refusing to enforce the 18th Amendment. In 1933, the 21st Amendment repealed prohibition, and the country was once again able to return to the public consumption of liquor. There was a brief surge in the production of Maryland rye after the repeal, but with the advent of World War II, grain and alcohol were diverted for military use. The popularity of blended whiskies grew as straight rye's suffered. As the demand for rye fell, even after the war, local distilleries started producing other spirits. Many simply closed. In 1972 the last rye whiskey was distilled in Maryland, and ten years later the last Maryland rye distiller packed up and left town. Majestic, producer of Pikesville Rye, was sold to Heaven Hill-Evan Williams, which continued production of Pikesville Rye, but in Kentucky. As it's no longer distilled in Maryland, Pikesville is now billed as a "Maryland-style" rye.

No doubt many a Maryland resident believes that Pikesville Rye is still made in-state. After all, the area of western Baltimore County known as Pikesville is still around and home to over 30,000 people. Alas, no rye whiskey has been cooked up in Maryland for decades. That is, not until Lyon

Distilling Company's Ben Lyon and Jaime Windon started mashing the first batch of Lyon Maryland Free State Rye Whiskey in the Eastern Shore town of St. Michael's. Maryland had been called the "Free State" since it adopted a new constitution in 1864 that abolished slavery. Re-coined by *Baltimore Sun* editor Hamilton Owens in 1923, the sobriquet "Free State" also refers to Maryland's Prohibition-related civil disobedience and was the perfect name for the state's first new rye in more than forty years.

Simply Amaizing

When summer comes to Maryland, people start clamoring for Silver Queen corn. A drive to Ocean City usually entails at least one stop at a roadside stand for a dozen or so ears of the sweet white stuff to boil up at one's destination, whether it be a condo on the beach or at home. In Maryland, Silver Queen *is* corn. And though some farm stands tout the stuff, real Silver Queen corn is a thing of the past. Commercial growers don't bother with it anymore, now that there are new and sweeter hybrids available like Aspen and Camelot. "Got any Whiteout (or Sugar Pearl or Country Gentleman)?" when asked of a farmer, just doesn't have the same ring to it. Not to mention that it sounds like a euphemism for something else entirely.

We call it corn, which comes from the early English word "corne" meaning any starchy grain. Each tribe of Native Americans had a different name for it, and while they sounded different, they all meant the same thing: "our mother," or, "she who sustains us." The tribes living in the piedmont and coastal plains of Maryland started cultivating corn around 1100 A.D. according to archeological evidence. It was not only the staff of life, but held symbolic and ritualistic significance to these tribes as well. All Christopher Columbus and his cronies knew for sure was that corn, or as they referred to it, *mahiz*, was not gold. Still, various explorers, from Dominican friars and Dutch merchants to English slave traders realized that the real value in *mahiz* was nutrition. By the time the first English settlers came to Maryland in the seventeenth century, corn had already made its way through Europe and was likely being grown in Asia and Africa as well.

The English brought wheat seed with them and planted it in the fertile soil around the Chesapeake. They did not realize that the hot summer would kill the grain meant to be grown in England's cooler and moister climate and had to resort to buying corn from the natives in order to survive. John Smith, who seemed to be one of the only truly smart people to come

©Thinkstock

to these shores at that time, paid close attention to the natives' farming techniques. He noticed that they planted squashes and pumpkins and set up watchtowers to guard the crops from hungry birds and vermin. He also noted that every village had a granary in which to store the harvested corn. Then he went back to his people and said, "Dummies! We need to grow our own corn!" (We're paraphrasing, of course.) And so they did. Smith's first cornfield, planted in Virginia in 1609, flourished, at least until he got sick and was sent back to London. Without him around to show everyone else how stupid they were, the colonists ate most of the corn; the rest spoiled or became rat chow. The Native Americans noticed and extorted the now weak English for muskets and gunpowder. Eventually, Earl de la Warr, aka Lord Delaware, swooped in and saved Virginia from themselves. John Smith's cornfield was replanted, and from then on, corn was one of the most important crops in the region.

Up in Maryland, the Calverts learned from Virginia's mistakes. Leonard Calvert, the first proprietary governor of the Maryland colony, worked it out with the Native Americans that his people would get half of the natives' corn crop. Between corn and tobacco, Marylanders, at least the plantation-owners, grew fat and happy.

Corn pone was a favorite of the Native Americans. They took dried corn and pounded it into a coarse meal. This was mixed with water and shaped into cakes that were then cooked on heated stones. The colonists learned to make these filling carbohydrate bombs, which they also called johnnycakes

Hominy Hominy Hominy

While many of us prefer to eat corn while it's still on the cob, steaming hot and slathered with butter, there were a couple generations of Marylanders who were big into hominy. Back in 1899, there were four hominy companies in business in the state. That doesn't seem like very many until you learn that there were only two fish companies, four oyster companies, and ten fruit companies (yet, oddly, five gold-mining companies) listed in the Annual Report of the Bureau of Industrial Statistics of Maryland for 1900. Created by a process known as nixtamalization, hominy is corn that has been cooked in an alkaline solution, washed, and hulled. The alkaline solution adds calcium and converts the bound niacin in the corn to free niacin, which is more readily absorbed by the human body. The technique was invented in Mesoamerica thousands of years ago and evidently spread to Native Americans in the Mid-Atlantic region sometime before the arrival of the Europeans. In the southwest United States, masa is probably the most common form of nixtamalized corn, and in the South, its grits, both products of which are dried and rehydrated forms. In Maryland, we like it wet—pearl hominy—which, these days, usually comes in a can bearing the brand Manning's.

Manning's started out as a home-canned product that was sold door-to-door. In 1917, the Manning family opened a small factory in the Canton neighborhood of Baltimore City and kept the place going for three generations. Now the company belongs to Lake Packing Company, located in Lottsburg, Virginia, just below the Maryland line, and a hop, skip, and a jump from the Chesapeake Bay.

and hoecakes. Popular mythology says that hoecakes were cooked over a gardening hoe held over an open fire, though in actuality, a hoe was a specific baking implement, much like a griddle or a peel.

But the corn that was grown back then wasn't quite the same thing as what we eat now. Sweet corn, the fat yellow or white kernels that we happily eat from cans, freezer bags, and of course on the cob, wasn't developed until the late 1700s and didn't gain in popularity until sometime after the Civil War. Field corn is edible too, of course, considering it sustained humans for many years before sweet corn came about. Sweet corn, *Zea mays saccharata*, is the result of a genetic mutation that controls the conversion of sugar to starch. It would have been too fussy a crop for the early Native Americans to maintain; "ripe" sweet corn must be picked when quite immature, in something called the "milk stage."

Today, we city dwellers tend to think of corn as something to eat on the Fourth of July, picked up at a local farm stand or farmers' market. Maryland corn, of course, is preferred. But out of the over 500,000 acres of corn planted on Maryland farms, the vast majority of it is field corn, which is used to make everything from animal feed to fuel to corn syrup. In 2014, the sweet corn that humans consume fresh provided only 2.7 percent of corn-related income in the state. Considering Maryland's 2014 corn crop was worth about $600 million, however, that's not insignificant. Still, cows reap more of the benefits of our Eastern Shore farms than we do.

Strawberry Fields Forever. Not.

Maryland has always been the land of boom or bust. If a farmer was successful growing one crop, he tended to stick to it. This lack of diversification meant that when one crop was no longer in favor, farmers had nothing to fall back on. In the cities, the same was true of industry. One or two large corporations employed thousands of workers, most of whom were uneducated and skilled only in very specific ways. When those corporations closed or left the area, the workers—and their children, some of whom had planned to go into their father's line of work—were left without jobs, and many were unsure of what to do next.

So we have the story of strawberries. In the early twentieth century, Marion Station, Maryland, was the strawberry shipping capital of the world. Buyers flocked to this town in Somerset County on Maryland's Eastern Shore each summer for strawberries grown there in Somerset, as well as

Worcester and Wicomico Counties. The berries, once purchased at the town's auction block, were then shipped in refrigerated railroad cars—sometimes hundreds of cars per day—to their destinations. The heart-shaped red berry that wears its ovaries on its skin was the leading source of income for the area's farmers back in the days before and during World War I. Most area farmers grew nothing else; they survived the winters on credit, hoping the next late-spring strawberry harvest would be better than the one before. The market peaked in 1918, with a quart of berries bringing as much as 30 cents. In the 1920s and 1930s, however, the market grew sour and more and more farmers went bankrupt. During the Great Depression (1929-39), strawberries were considered a luxury item, despite selling for as little as a nickel a quart. Today, much of the land that once grew strawberries supports chicken factories.

The strawberry industry in Maryland is far from dead. While it's not exactly booming or even close to producing the numbers of berries and dollars as in the early part of the last century, the US Department of Agriculture's 2012 census showed that about 220 acres of strawberries were grown on 187 farms, many of which are of the "pick your own," variety. Some of these farms, particularly those on the Western Shore of the Chesapeake, originally grew tobacco. Thanks to Maryland's tobacco buyout program, some farmers were able to successfully transition from growing one income-producing product to another.

Strawberries are low-growing perennials, and make a fine crop for farmers with small plots of land. Most of Maryland's strawberries are June-bearing, meaning they produce the largest crops in June, before the stinky heat of a Maryland summer really sets in. Another type of cultivar, known as day-neutral, has two peak growing seasons: June, and late summer until the end of the growing season. But as with most crops, strawberries drain nutrients from the soil and must be planted in different fields every few years to give the land a rest.

It's likely that the produce farms of Somerset County will never be as lucrative as they were in the past, but the county does have a place in the annals of produce history. John Wesley Nelson, born in Crisfield in 1852, left Somerset County as a teen, made his way to Baltimore, then to Chicago, and finally settled in California. He got a job working for a small fruit grower and enjoyed the work so much, he later bought the company. Today Del Monte Foods is one of the largest branded food producers in the United States.

In a Nutshell

Black walnut trees aren't exactly a farm crop in Maryland, but they do play an important part in protecting water quality. You know those annoying plum-sized mid-green blobs that end up on your lawn, the ones that squirrels tear open to leave dark brown sooty stains on your driveway? Inside those green fruits are black walnuts, a delicious but difficult treat.

It must have been a very hungry and very determined person who cracked open and enjoyed the first black walnut. The idiom, "a tough nut to crack," is certainly true; these nuts are not exactly snacks one can enjoy while watching a ballgame.

The black walnut tree, or *Juglans nigra*, is native to Maryland, to much of the Atlantic seaboard, and as far west as eastern Texas. Not only do these trees produce a delicious nut, similar to its cousin the English walnut, but with a muskier, darker flavor, they also produce a desirable hardwood. Black walnut wood is tough and strong, but because it is less dense than oak, it's also easy to work. In the colonial days, black walnut was plentiful and used extensively in furniture-making, even being exported back to England for use there. In the 1880s, the wood fell out of favor, but with the advent of World War I, there was a resurgence, when it was used in gunstocks and airplane propellers.

© Thinkstock

Harvesting Black Walnuts

If you don't have enough nuts to donate, then by all means eat them. The first step in enjoying your home-grown black walnuts is to remove the husk. That brown stuff inside stains and can be used as a dye, so wear gloves. Discard the husks and dry the nuts in a well-ventilated place for a few weeks. The dryer the nut, the easier to crack. (Perhaps the first step in the process is actually to have patience.) After that time, toss out any nuts that look moldy, and get out the safety goggles and vise. First, put on the goggles—a chunk of flying walnut shell in the eye is too high a price to pay even for the deliciousness of black walnuts. Then put the nut in the vise with the seam parallel to the jaws, and apply pressure until the nut splits open. If you don't have goggles handy, you can put a bath towel over the whole shebang, to catch errant fragments. Once the nut is cracked, use a nut pick to pry out the meat.

Today, trees large enough to cut for their desirable lumber are scarcer, partly because it takes so long for them to grow to a reasonable size. There are even black walnut poachers out there who sneak onto properties and cut down trees without authorization. Chances are the black walnut trees that are in your area aren't of lumber quality, but they still produce those annoying nuts. You can do the Chesapeake Bay a service by gathering those nuts for the Maryland Forest Service. They're husked and planted in nurseries, and a couple years later, the seedlings are re-planted in Washington and Frederick Counties as part of Maryland's Stream ReLeaf Program. The trees provide stream bank stabilization, erosion control, and improve wildlife habitats, and their roots help buffer pollutants in rainwater. While neither county is near the Bay, ultimately, most of the waterways in the state drain into the Chesapeake.

You Say "Tomahto," But I'd Rather Eat Them

The tomato is a New World fruit. Discovered by Spanish explorers in the fifteenth century, tomatoes were introduced to Europe, the Caribbean, and the Philippines well before they were used as a food product in the English-settled Chesapeake Bay region. For many years, they were believed to be poisonous and unfit for consumption. While tomatoes are a member of the deadly nightshade family, and contain small amounts of the poisonous alkaloid *tomatine*, they are quite safe to eat. And as we all know, very delicious.

It wasn't until the early 1800s that tomatoes were grown in Maryland for culinary purposes. A century later, Maryland was among the top tomato producing states. New Jersey, eat your heart out.

Growing up in Maryland as late as the 1960s, we enjoyed our share of fat, flavorful, locally grown tomatoes. Everyone knew that fresh tomatoes could only be enjoyed seasonally, and that they tasted best when just picked off the vine, or at the very least, when newly purchased from a roadside vegetable vendor, preferably on the Eastern Shore. The rest of the year, pale pink supermarket tomatoes just didn't cut it.

But the history of tomatoes in Maryland is not just about fresh produce. Not only were there plenty of delicious nightshades grown on the shores of the Chesapeake, but a large majority of them were canned in Maryland, too. While Baltimore was the canning capital of the country for a while, by the early twentieth century the city of Cambridge, in Dorchester County on the Eastern Shore, was known as the "tomato canning capital of the world." Wicomico County, too, was known for growing and canning tomatoes. The soil in Wicomico, coupled with the long growing season, was especially favorable for growing tomatoes.

Canneries popped up in Wicomico County and all along the Eastern Shore. At one point there were 300 of them operating in the area. Though the conditions were quite harsh, the new industry was a godsend for Maryland, which by the beginning of the last century, was teeming with recent immigrants who needed jobs. At least one of our Polish-born grandmothers spent humid Maryland summers ankle-deep in tomato juice while working as a skinner, young children at her side. The locals, too, would do seasonal cannery work to make extra income. The canneries thrived into mid-century, but by the 1970s, had dwindled down to a handful. The amount of tomatoes grown in the state declined as well, from 51,000 acres in the 1930s to less than 1,000 in the early 2000s.

The good news for tomato lovers is that tomatoes are easy to grow, flourishing in both garden plots and back porch containers. So while the tomato industry in Maryland isn't what it used to be, anyone with a balcony and some potting soil can still enjoy a fresh and juicy Maryland-grown tomato in the summertime.

The Future of Chesapeake Products – Lyon Distilling

Despite Maryland once ranking second only to Kentucky in spirits production, few people today seem to want to bother with making hard liquor. There are world-class microbreweries all over the state, from western Maryland to the Eastern Shore, but just a handful of brave folks entering the new wilderness of distilling. Not that it's new, in and of itself, but as the last Maryland distillery closed in the waning years of the twentieth century, it's been quite a long time since that particular art form, if you will, has been explored in the state.

Ben Lyon and business partner Jaime Windon started Lyon Distilling a handful of years ago with the notion of bringing the fine art of alcohol back to Maryland. After developing several rums and a moonshine corn whiskey, they set about to tackle a rye. Ben said, "I'm sort of never satisfied with a surface level look at anything, so I've had the tendency to go down the road exploring genres. Jamie and I started to get into rye. We knew rye had a very interesting Maryland history and a mystery that surrounds the disappearance of Maryland rye. It's historically significant but also something we love."

One of the remarkable things they discovered about Maryland-style rye was that there was no set mix of ingredients, known as the mash bill, for making it. Therefore, Ben set out to make a mix that was satisfying to him. "It would be nice to redefine the genre, because it's absolutely gone. I like low-rye-content rye. My goal is to make an exceptionally complex and balanced rye. Rye is more interesting than bourbon . . . appley doughy notes. . . corn doesn't really create these notes on its own. [And] there's a cereal note from barley that rounds things out nicely."

To be called rye whiskey, the liquor needs to adhere to certain governmental requirements. It must be made from a grain mixture that is no less than 51 percent rye aged in new, charred-oak barrels and distilled to no more than 160 proof. The finished, bottled rye must be no less than 80 proof. Lyon uses 55 percent rye, 35 percent corn, and 10 percent malted barley, ending up with a robust 90 proof product.

Rye whiskey is a temperamental product to create. Overheat the mixture, for example, and the polysaccharides will turn into superglue. These difficulties are even more pronounced for small-batch distilleries. "It's a personal challenge," Ben said. "We didn't want to do a typical 95–100 percent rye like what is on the market. There are a lot of one-dimensional ryes out there. I wanted to replicate a low-rye-content rye, because it's what a Maryland rye is. Very nicely balanced, with spice and depth and complexity, but it doesn't catch you at the back of the throat. It's an important style of rye to do. It's really nice to sip and have in cocktails. It adds another dimension."

We were allowed to taste the rye whiskey before it was placed in New American Oak Number 3 char barrels for aging. Even in its "white" stage, the rye already exhibited grassy, earthy spice notes along with a tobacco-y, caramel-y finish. The rye gains even more complexity as it absorbs the flavors of the barrels.

Although they are well on their way to mastering a fine rye whiskey, Ben does not want to stop there. "Being a distiller isn't glamorous. Seventy percent of it is cleaning stuff and moving heavy things around. I don't want to have it become a grind, or to get stuck in a rut." To that end, Lyon Distillery is working on creating a malt whiskey next. He's also working with local breweries like Union Craft Brewing in Baltimore and R&R Brewing in Cambridge to create spirits distilled with beers.

With so many new businesses emphasizing the word "craft," we asked Ben what the term means to him. "In any industry, there's a gold standard, a pinnacle of achievement. In distilling, it's that you start with raw ingredients, you go through mashing, fermentation, distillation, and bottling." He then added, "The only thing that matters is what the consumer thinks. If they think 'craft' matters, then it matters."

© Kathy Wielech Patterson

B&O Old Fashioned

COURTESY OF BRENDAN DORR, B & O AMERICAN BRASSERIE

The Old Fashioned is a classic drink that requires whiskey, bitters, and sugar. Head bartender at the B&O American Brasserie, Brendan Dorr, uses crème de cacao as the sugary element in this drink. He also enhances the drink's flavors with a bit of Amaro and a pinch of scotch to make the best Old Fashioned you've ever had.
(MAKES 1 DRINK)

2 ounces rye whiskey

½ ounce Tempus Fugit crème de cacao

½ ounce Amaro Nonino

1 barspoon Laphroig 10-year-old scotch

2 dashes Abbott's bitters

Strip of orange peel

Combine all ingredients in a mixing glass and stir with ice. Strain into a rocks glass filled with large-format ice. Garnish with orange peel.

Black Walnut Cake

It's funny to read old recipes, particularly the ones consisting merely of a list of ingredients. It was assumed that the person cooking or baking must know the proper techniques, because more often than not, what we consider important details like oven temperature or pan sizes were omitted. Such is the case with many old recipes for black walnut cake. Judging by the ingredients, the traditional version was a pound cake (because it contained about a pound each of butter, flour, and sugar) and was most likely pretty dense. Here's a modernized version of a black walnut pound cake, made lighter by the use of leavening—and less than a pound of the remaining ingredients.

(SERVES 10–12)

8 ounces unsalted butter

1 cup sugar

4 eggs

1 teaspoon vanilla

2 cups all-purpose flour

1 teaspoon baking powder

¼ teaspoon salt

½ teaspoon freshly grated nutmeg

1½ cups black walnut pieces

Preheat oven to 350°F. Grease a 9 x 5-inch loaf pan and set aside.

Put the butter and sugar into the bowl of a stand mixer and beat on medium speed until pale. Scrape down bowl and add eggs, one at a time, beating until each is well incorporated before adding the next. Stir in the vanilla.

In a separate bowl, whisk together the flour, baking powder, salt, and nutmeg. Turn mixer speed to low and add the flour mixture. Beat only until flour is incorporated; don't overmix. Turn off mixer and stir in walnuts by hand, scraping bottom and sides of bowl to get any unmixed flour.

Scrape the batter into the prepared pan. Bake for about an hour, or until a toothpick inserted into the middle of the cake comes out clean. If the cake appears to be browning too quickly, tent it loosely with foil.

Allow cake to cool in pan set on a wire rack for at least half an hour before unmolding.

Black Walnut Scones with Bleu Cheese and Figs

Black walnuts have an underlying funkiness, somewhat akin to the funk of bleu cheese; therefore, they are a perfect pairing. The addition of dried figs adds a bit of complementary sweetness. Terrific with strong black tea, we also like these scones for breakfast with a cup of coffee.

(SERVES 8)

8–10 dried figs

2 cups all-purpose flour

⅔ cup black walnut pieces

½ cup crumbled bleu cheese

1 tablespoon baking powder

½ teaspoon salt

4 ounces cold unsalted butter, cut into small pieces

¾ cup heavy cream, plus more for brushing tops

Preheat oven to 450°F.

Stem the figs and cut them into small dice. Toss with a tablespoon of the flour, making sure every sticky bit of fig has been separated by some flour. Combine with the walnuts and bleu cheese and set aside.

In a large bowl, combine the rest of the flour, the baking powder, and salt. Using your fingers, blend in the butter until the mixture resembles coarse meal. Stir in the cream, figs, walnuts, and cheese and mix only until dry ingredients have been moistened. Don't overwork, or the scones will be tough.

Turn mixture out onto a lightly floured work surface. Pat gently into an 8-inch round. Cut into eight wedges. Place each wedge on a parchment-covered baking sheet. Brush tops with a bit of heavy cream.

Bake for 15 minutes, or until golden.

© Kathy Wielech Patters

Corn Bread

COURTESY OF CHEF ZACK MILLS, WIT & WISDOM

Corn pone was a staple food for Native Americans, and the colonists adopted it as well. Eventually, with the introduction of leavening agents like baking powder and baking soda, the stick-to-your-ribs pone became a lighter and airier cake-like substance we call corn bread. Popular throughout the south, corn bread is also a perfect accompaniment to Maryland favorites like fried chicken and crab soup. Chef Mills' version has an unexpected hint of citrus, the flavor of which can cut the richness of any meaty foods it may be served with. It would also make a stellar base for a strawberry shortcake-style dessert.
(MAKES ABOUT 20 PIECES)

8 ounces unsalted butter, at room temperature

1 teaspoon orange zest

1 teaspoon lemon zest

1 cup sugar

1 tablespoon salt

4 large eggs, at room temperature

1¼ cups yellow cornmeal

1 cup all-purpose flour

¾ teaspoon of baking soda

8 ounces sour cream

Preheat oven to 350°F.

Using a stand mixer with whisk attachment, cream the butter with the zest, sugar, and salt until fully combined. Slowly add the eggs, one at a time, while beating the mixture on medium-low speed. Scrape down the bowl occasionally with a spatula. Once the eggs have been integrated, add the cornmeal.

Sift the flour and baking soda together and add it to the batter. Mix until about halfway combined, then add the sour cream and beat until fully incorporated.

Line the bottom of a 9 x 12-inch baking pan with parchment and spray with release spray. Spread batter evenly. Bake for about 20 minutes, until lightly golden brown.

Buttered Corn on the Cob Soup with Corn and Crab Salad

COURTESY OF CHEF CHAD WELLS, ALEWIFE

This soup should be smooth, like a bisque, so don't omit the straining steps to remove the corn kernel skins. It can be served cold or hot, with or without the crab salad.
(MAKES 10 SERVINGS)

For the soup:

8 ears of corn

Blended oil

1½ onions, roughly chopped

6 stalks of celery, roughly chopped

Kosher salt

6 ounces unsalted butter

6 ounces flour

1 quart heavy cream

1½ tablespoons Old Bay® Seasoning

Sugar (optional)

For the crab salad:

2 ears of corn

1 jalapeno pepper, diced (seeds removed, if you wish)

4 tomatoes, seeded and diced

½ onion, diced

½ bunch cilantro, minced

Juice of 1 lime

Splash extra virgin olive oil

Salt to taste

6 ounces lump crab meat, picked over for shells

© Jay Fleming

To make the soup: Remove the corn kernels from the ears of corn and set aside. In a very large pot, add a couple tablespoons of the blended oil. Put in the onions, celery, and corn cobs, and cook, stirring regularly, until the vegetables start to soften. Pour in about a gallon of water, or enough to cover the corn cobs. Bring to a boil, then turn down to a simmer and cook for about 2 hours. At that time, taste the broth and salt vigorously. The stock should taste very corny.

Strain the stock and set aside.

Melt the butter in a large pot and stir in the flour. Continue to stir until the flour and butter are completely incorporated and start to smell slightly toasty; do not brown. Whisk in the reserved corn stock, then add the cream and the reserved corn kernels. Cook over medium heat until the soup has thickened somewhat. Using a stick blender, puree the corn as smoothly as possible. Strain the soup once more and place back over the heat. Simmer over low heat for about 45 minutes. Season with Old Bay® Seasoning and additional salt, if needed. If the corn wasn't particularly sweet, you can add a bit of sugar to help it out.

To make the salad: Husk the corn and place the cobs directly on a grill to char the kernels all over. Alternatively, you can char the kernels over a gas burner on your stove. Allow to cool, then cut the kernels off the cobs.

Toss the kernels with the jalapeno, tomato, onion, and cilantro. Season with the lime juice, a bit of olive oil, and salt to taste. Gently fold in the crab.

To serve: Ladle soup into bowls. Add a dollop of the crab salad in the center. Sprinkle additional Old Bay® Seasoning over the soup, if desired.

Corn Fritters

Adapted from Singing Valleys, these go very well with fried chicken, as in the Escoffier version of Chicken à la Maryland (see page 155).
(MAKES 8-12, DEPENDING ON SIZE)

4 ounces butter, melted and cooled

3 large eggs

1 cup flour, sifted

1 teaspoons salt

1 teaspoons black pepper

2 cups fresh corn kernels

Oil for frying

Combine the butter and eggs in a large bowl and beat well to combine. Whisk in the flour and seasonings, then stir in the corn.

Heat a half-inch or so of oil in a cast iron pan or other heavy pot. Drop spoonfuls of batter into the hot oil and fry until crisp and brown on both sides. Drain on paper towel–lined plates and serve hot.

Sweet Corn Ice Cream with Blueberry Compote and Caramel Popcorn

COURTESY OF CHEF SCOTT HINES, B&O AMERICAN BRASSERIE

Corn is an incredible versatile ingredient. Not only can it be used in savory applications, but also in sweet ones, as in this ice cream–based dessert.
(MAKES 5–6 SERVINGS)

For ice cream:

2 ears corn

1 cup heavy cream

1½ cups milk

½ cup sugar

4 large egg yolks

½ teaspoon vanilla extract

For popcorn:

1 cup sugar

½ cup heavy cream

2 cups popped popcorn

For the compote:

2 cups fresh blueberries

1 cup sugar

1 sprig fresh thyme

1 teaspoon fresh lemon juice

To make ice cream: Using the large hole side of a box grater, grate corn off the cob into a bowl, retaining all juices. Place the corn and juices and both cream and milk into a saucepan set over medium heat and warm gently.

In a bowl, whisk together sugar and egg yolks until thick. When the corn cream mixture comes to a simmer, whisk some of it into the egg mixture to temper the eggs. Pour the tempered eggs into the saucepan with the remaining corn cream and, whisking constantly, heat until thickened. Make sure it doesn't boil, otherwise you'll end up with scrambled eggs. Remove from heat and stir in the vanilla. Pour into a bowl. Cover bowl with a sheet of plastic wrap, pressing the plastic onto the surface of the custard to prevent a skin from forming. Chill for at least 2 hours.

Once chilled, pour into an ice cream maker and freeze according to manufacturer's directions.

To make popcorn: Put sugar and half cup water into a heavy saucepan and cook over medium heat without stirring until golden brown. Turn heat up and whisk in cream. Because it's cold, the cream will cause the caramel to seize up; just continue whisking until the mixture is smooth again. Bring to a boil, then turn off the heat.

Put the popcorn into a bowl and pour the caramel over, tossing to coat. Spread out on a parchment-lined baking sheet and set aside to firm up. When cooled, break popcorn up into small chunks.

To make compote: Combine fruit and sugar in a saucepan and allow to macerate at room temperature for 20 minutes. Add the thyme to the pot and cook the mixture over medium heat for 10 minutes, until sugar has melted completely and sauce has thickened. Remove the thyme and stir in the lemon juice. Refrigerate in a covered container until ready to serve.

To serve: Scoop ice cream into bowls. Top with blueberry compote and caramel popcorn.

Crab Posole Soup

These days, it seems that hominy is seen far more often in its dried and ground form—grits—than otherwise. And while grits are lovely, especially when paired with shrimp in a classic Louisiana dish, we think wet, or pearl, hominy deserves a place in the sun as well. Wet hominy is far more "corny" flavored than the ground stuff, and while it tastes of corn, the texture is far starchier. Cooked simply with fried onions and a healthy dose of salt and pepper, hominy is delicious, but it's also mighty fine in this twist on a traditional Mexican hominy dish, *pozole*.
(SERVES 6–8)

1 pound tomatillos

1–2 fresh jalapeno peppers

½ cup cilantro, including stems (divided use)

1 tablespoon olive oil

1 large onion, chopped

1 teaspoon kosher salt

4 garlic cloves, crushed

4 cups seafood stock or clam juice

2 (15-ounce) cans white hominy, preferably Manning's, drained and rinsed

1 tablespoon agave syrup, or to taste

¼ teaspoon ground coriander

Large pinch ground cumin

½ pound backfin crabmeat, picked over for shells

1 avocado, peeled, seeded, and sliced

Sour cream

1 lime, cut into wedges

Husk and rinse the tomatillos. Core and quarter them and place into a blender. Remove stems and some or all of the seeds from the jalapenos (depending on how much heat you want) and place them in the blender with the tomatillos. Add half of the cilantro and puree. You may need to add a little water to facilitate blending. Set aside.

Heat oil in a large saucepan over medium high heat. Add onion and salt and saute until tender, about 5 minutes. Add garlic and cook for another minutes or so, stirring constantly. Add the tomatillo/jalapeno puree and cook for an additional 3 to 4 minutes. Pour in the seafood stock or clam juice and hominy and bring to a boil. Turn heat to a steady simmer and cook for 30 minutes, stirring occasionally.

At the end of the 30 minutes, stir in the agave syrup, coriander, and cumin. Gently stir in the crab. Remove soup from the heat and ladle into bowls. Top each serving with some of the avocado, a dollop of sour cream, and the remaining cilantro. Serve with lime wedges.

© Kathy Wielech Patterson

The Best Way to Eat a Maryland Tomato

If you've never tried this, you're doing yourself a disservice. Tomato sandwiches are perfect for breakfast, lunch, dinner, or snacks.
(SERVES 1)

1 ripe tomato

Kosher salt

2 slices good-quality white bread

Mayonnaise

Core and slice the tomato into ½-inch-thick slices. Sprinkle a bit of salt on the tomato. Spread both slices of bread on one side with as much or as little of the mayonnaise as you like. Arrange the tomato on one piece of bread, then top with the second piece of bread. Eat. Repeat as often as necessary.

© Thinksto

Caramelized Tomato Shortcake

Mrs. Mary Rattley, a native of Southern Maryland, was chief cook in the Herbert Hoover household for the eight years he served as Secretary of Commerce under Presidents Harding and Coolidge. One of Hoover's favorite dishes, according to Rattley, was her "caramel tomatoes." (He was also a big fan of shad and shad roe.) "You cut off the tops of the tomatoes—leave the stem—and make a cavity in the top, and fill each hole with a good-sized piece of butter—not a stingy piece—and put a tablespoonful of sugar on each tomato. Sprinkle with salt, and put in the oven to cook until the sugar is brown and the tomato done but not flat. Stick a sprig of parsley in the top of each tomato and serve on rounds of toast with sauce of the tomato. That makes a very pretty dish." The resulting tomatoes are almost sweet enough to eat for dessert.

Rather than serve entire large tomatoes, we prefer to lightly caramelize plum tomato halves, balancing out the sweet with a bit of vinegar. This dish, when paired with a green salad, makes a nice lunch. It can also be used as an appetizer.
(SERVES 6)

For tomatoes:

6 plum tomatoes

2 cloves garlic, crushed

2 tablespoons extra virgin olive oil

1 tablespoon sherry vinegar

2 tablespoons packed brown sugar

1 teaspoon kosher salt

For onions:

½ red onion, thinly sliced

2 tablespoons olive oil

Pinch salt

For shortcake:

1½ cups all-purpose flour

½ cup cornmeal

¼ cup sugar

1 teaspoon baking powder

1 teaspoon baking soda

¼ teaspoon salt

½ cup cold unsalted butter, cut into small pieces

½ cup milk

For cream:

1 cup chilled whipping cream

2 teaspoons finely grated lemon zest

1 tablespoon finely minced fresh basil

Pinch cayenne pepper

Pinch salt

Basil for garnish

To make tomatoes: Preheat oven to 450°F degrees. Cut tomatoes in half lengthwise, scoop out and discard the seeds. Arrange the tomatoes, cut side up, on a parchment-lined baking sheet. Sprinkle with the garlic. Combine oil, vinegar, brown sugar, and salt in a bowl and drizzle over tomatoes. Bake until tomatoes are softened and caramelized, about 30 minutes. Set aside to cool.

To make onions: Cook onions in olive oil and a pinch of salt over medium-low heat until very soft, about 30 minutes.

To make shortcake: Preheat oven to 350°F. Grease a six-cup muffin tin.

In a medium bowl, combine flour, cornmeal, sugar, baking powder, baking soda, and salt. Using your fingers or a pastry blender, rub in butter until mixture resembles coarse crumbs. Add milk, stirring just until mixed.

Divide the dough into six balls (it will be very sticky) and place one into each greased muffin cup. Bake 20 to 25 minutes or until browned on top. Remove from muffin tin and allow to cool on a wire rack until ready to use.

To make cream: Place whipping cream in a cold bowl. With an electric mixer, start beating it on low speed until it starts to thicken. Increase the speed to medium and whip until very thick but before stiff peaks form. Stir in the lemon, basil, cayenne, and salt. Cover and refrigerate until ready to use, up to 1 hour.

To assemble cakes: Split cooled shortcakes in half lengthwise. Add a dollop of the whipped cream to the bottom cake, then a spoonful of onions and two tomato halves. Top with the other half of the shortcake and another dollop of cream. Garnish with basil.

Mediterranean Bread Salad

This is a tomato recipe, but it's also a good way to introduce the Maryland beaten biscuit, the recipe for which follows this one.

In Italy and the Middle East, stale bread is often used as a salad component, tossed with tomatoes and cucumbers and a sprightly vinaigrette. The Italian version is called *panzanella*, and in the Levant, it's *fattoush*. Maryland beaten biscuits, with their firm texture, don't even need to be stale to make a delicious salad. Split and toasted, they are akin to hearty croutons. You can use them as is, untoasted, but keep in mind that they will soak up more dressing that way. If you don't have the biscuits, you can use 2 cups of slightly stale crusty bread, torn into rough 1- to 2-inch chunks.

Sumac is a spice made from dried red berries. It has a tangy, somewhat lemony flavor. It can be found in Middle Eastern markets, but it's not absolutely necessary for this vinegar. Pomegranate molasses, as well, is a Middle Eastern ingredient. You can use ¾ tablespoon of honey, instead, and omit the superfine sugar.

(SERVES 6)

Kathy Wielech Patterson

For the dressing:

2 tablespoons fresh lemon juice

1 tablespoon pomegranate molasses

1 large garlic clove, minced

1 tablespoon red wine vinegar

1 teaspoon ground sumac (optional)

1 teaspoon superfine sugar

¼ cup extra virgin olive oil

Kosher salt and freshly ground pepper

For the salad:

10 Maryland beaten biscuits

3 cups chopped tomato or halved cherry tomatoes

1 large cucumber, peeled, quartered lengthwise, and cut into ¼-inch chunks

¼ cup kalamata olives, pitted and quartered

2 scallions, chopped

1 cup parsley, chopped

½ cup chopped fresh mint

½ cup crumbled feta cheese

To make dressing: Combine lemon juice, pomegranate molasses, garlic, vinegar, sumac, and sugar in a small bowl. Whisk in oil gradually. Season with salt and pepper to taste.

To make salad: Cut biscuits in half and toast until lightly browned. Break toasted biscuits into chunks and place into a large bowl. Add tomatoes, cucumbers, olives, and scallions and toss with the dressing. Add the parsley, mint, and feta and toss again.

Maryland Beaten Biscuits

Sadly, this traditional Maryland baked good seems to have gone the way of the dodo. Beaten biscuits, popular in the South, were a good way for cooks to vent their frustrations, build their biceps, or both. The dough was indeed beaten, smacked but good with the side of a rolling pin, a hammer, or as one recipe found in *Maryland's Way* calls for, a hatchet. Some have postulated that smacking the dough around incorporates air in the absence of leavening. Indeed, many recipes suggest that the beating be done until the surface of the dough is blistered, indicating surface air pockets. Others say that working the dough so much severs the long strands of gluten ordinarily formed when a dough is made; the fat in the biscuits coats the broken strands and keeps them from reforming. We are more inclined to go with the latter explanation, as the final product has a very close, dense, texture that is the antithesis of airy.

In the latter part of the nineteenth century, a hand-cranked machine that rolled the dough much like a pasta machine was employed. The biscuit break saved a lot of arm strength, but probably wasn't gentle on the wrists. Eventually, the electric food processor made things much easier, but fans of the old ways will likely shake their heads and tell you it's just "not the same."

A well-made beaten biscuit should be soft yet firm, with a lightly crisp crust, not hard or tough, and fairly pale in color. The biscuits are round, a little bit bigger than a golf ball but with a flattened bottom, and a characteristic pricked pattern on top. Some bakers used a fork, but others had special pricking tools made for them that were then passed down through the generations.

While the biscuits are tasty when fresh from the oven, they serve their purpose when stale, too. Hard beaten biscuits can be broken up and added to a bowl of soup, much like an oyster cracker, or blitzed into crumbs to use like any other bread crumbs.

(MAKES ABOUT 30 BISCUITS)

4½ cups all-purpose flour

1 teaspoon Kosher salt

4 ounces shortening or butter

Preheat oven to 325°F.

Combine flour and salt in a large bowl. Rub in the butter until mixture resembles coarse meal. Gradually stir in 1½ cups of cold water. Remove dough from the bowl and knead a few times on a lightly floured surface, then form into a stiff ball.

Flatten the ball by smacking it with a rolling pin or other heavy blunt object. Continuously beat the dough, folding it onto itself occasionally, for 30 to 45 minutes, until the surface is blistered and the dough is smooth and elastic. Alternatively, divide the dough in half and beat each in a food

Kathy Wielech Patterson

processor equipped with a dough blade for two minutes in 30-second bursts with about a minute in between, so the processor and dough don't get overheated. Remove from the processor, combine the two halves, and roll and fold the dough several times until smooth-looking.

Pull off golf ball-sized pieces of dough and roll into balls. Place them evenly spaced on ungreased baking sheets. Prick the tops decoratively with the tines of a fork and bake for about 40 minutes, until just lightly browned on the bottoms. The tops should remain very light.

Use a fork or the point of a knife to split the biscuits and serve warm with butter or cold with thin slices of cured ham.

Strawberry Chopped Salad

This pretty salad is both light and substantial. It's nice as a starter or a side dish, but pair it with a black walnut bleu cheese and fig scone for a perfect springtime lunch.

Taste your strawberries before proceeding with the dressing. If your berries are very sweet, then use less honey or agave syrup, but if they are quite tart, you will need more. (SERVES 4–6)

For the dressing:

1 teaspoon to 1 tablespoon honey or agave syrup

1 teaspoon Dijon mustard

Generous pinch kosher salt

Several grinds fresh black pepper

¼ teaspoon ancho chile powder

1 tablespoon balsamic vinegar

1 tablespoon rice wine vinegar

2 tablespoons extra virgin olive oil

For the salad:

1 pint strawberries, hulled and diced

1 medium cucumber, peeled, seeded, and diced

4 teaspoons minced red onion

6 leaves romaine lettuce, chopped

¼ cup crumbled bleu cheese

2 tablespoons chopped roasted almonds, pecans, or walnuts, or a combination

2 tablespoons finely chopped fresh basil

2 tablespoons finely chopped fresh mint

To make the dressing: Put honey or agave and mustard in a small bowl and beat vigorously with a fork or small whisk. Add the salt, pepper, chile powder, and vinegar and whisk again. Drizzle in the olive oil, whisking continuously, until emulsified.

To make the salad: Combine the salad ingredients except for the basil and mint in a large bowl. Give the dressing another quick whisking and pour over the fruit and vegetables, tossing to coat. Add the herbs and toss again. Serve immediately.

© Kathy Wielech Patterson

Haussner's Strawberry Pie

Haussner's was a Baltimore restaurant known for many things, among them the fine art that lined the walls, the abundant bread basket, and the strawberry pie. That pie seemed like a pretty simple affair—flaky crust, pastry cream, strawberries—but it's actually more complicated than that. We took it upon ourselves to recreate the pie at home, modifying the recipes we found on the Internet to produce what, in our memory, is pretty close to the original Haussner's Strawberry Pie.
(SERVES 6–8)

For strawberry glaze:

1 cup water

¾ cup granulated sugar

½ teaspoon natural strawberry extract

2 tablespoons cornstarch

2 tablespoons cold water

For pastry cream:

6 egg yolks

⅔ cup granulated sugar

4 tablespoons cornstarch, sifted

3 tablespoons flour, sifted

2 cups whole milk

4 tablespoons unsalted butter

1 teaspoon vanilla

To assemble pie:

1 tablespoon sliced almonds

1 pre-baked 9-inch pie shell, can be homemade or store-bought

2 pints of large strawberries

Freshly whipped cream

To make strawberry glaze: Combine water, sugar, and strawberry extract in a saucepan and bring to a boil over medium heat until the sugar is completely dissolved.

In a small bowl, mix together the cornstarch and cold water until cornstarch is dissolved. Pour the cornstarch into the boiling sugar water and cook, stirring often, until the glaze is transparent, about 3 minutes. Remove glaze from the heat and allow to cool to room temperature.

To make the pastry cream: Using an electric mixer, beat the egg yolks and sugar until they are light and lemon-colored. Combine the cornstarch and flour. Gradually add it to the egg yolks in the mixer and continue to beat until smooth, scraping down the bowl occasionally.

Put the milk into a saucepan and heat until steam starts to rise from the surface and tiny bubbles appear around the edges. Remove from heat and pour into a measuring cup with a spout.

While the mixer is still running, carefully drizzle the hot milk into the egg mixture. When milk has been completely incorporated, transfer mixture to a saucepan and bring to a boil, whisking constantly. After a couple of minutes, the mixture will thicken considerably; at that point remove it from the heat and stir in the butter and vanilla.

© Kathy Wielech Patterson

Strain the pastry cream into a bowl and chill it for 1 hour. To prevent a skin from forming, place a buttered round of waxed paper on top. Makes about 3 cups.

To assemble: Toast the almonds in a dry skillet, stirring regularly, until lightly browned and fragrant, about 2 minutes. Remove to a plate and set aside.

Spread the pastry cream into the prepared pie shell.

Wash and dry all of the strawberries and slice off the hulls. Put aside the biggest and best-looking berries. Place the remaining berries in a large bowl and pour some of the glaze over them. Gently toss to coat, being careful not to bruise the fruit. Arrange a single layer of glazed strawberries, points up, around the perimeter of the pie. Cut some of the glazed berries in half and place, cut-side-down, on the custard, to fill the center. Add the reserved large berries to the bowl and pour on more glaze. Arrange these remaining berries in concentric circles over the cut berries, with the largest ones toward the center.

Put the whipped cream into a piping bag with a star tip. Pipe a 1-inch wide halo of cream about 4 inches in diameter on top of the pie. Sprinkle whipped cream with toasted almonds.

Refrigerate pie for at least 1 hour before serving.

A Chicken in Every Pot

When the first shiploads of English settlers came to these shores, they brought flocks of chickens with them. The European fowl helped the colonists survive their early years in the New World, but fell out of favor when the settlers realized that tastier game birds, like turkey and duck, were plentiful here. After a while, chickens were considered so unimportant that slaves were allowed to own them. But when black cooks began to make dishes like fried chicken for their masters, the appetite for the flightless fowl was whetted once again. Still, pork and beef remained the more popular proteins for many years.

In the nineteenth and twentieth centuries, millions of European Jews immigrated to the United States. Chicken played a large part in their cuisine, and soon poultry production increased to meet the demand. Much of

Thinkstock

the chicken in those days came from the Midwest, where rural women raised the birds for eggs and meat to sell or trade. This was true of farmwomen in Maryland as well. Chickens primarily served to put eggs or meat on the table, but occasionally old hens and young cockerels were sold or used as barter for household goods. When the shore region's usual cash crops—like strawberries and tomatoes—fell upon hard times due to insects, drought, or falling farm commodities prices, chickens became a valuable resource. But it wasn't until World War II, when beef and pork were reserved for the troops, that a billion-dollar industry was truly in the making.

In 2013, the state of Maryland was ranked eighth in the nation in both the number of broiler chickens produced and their value—just under one billion dollars. Tyson Foods, one of the top chicken producers in the country, has facilities on the Eastern Shore. But thanks to the pervasive influence of television, those of us who have grown up in the Mid-Atlantic region are perhaps more familiar with Perdue Farms.

Arthur W. Perdue was working for the railroad when he noticed that the egg farms popping up all over the Delmarva Peninsula after World War I were producing not only chickens but also income. He decided to get into the act himself, raising his brood in his backyard near Salisbury, Maryland. At first, Perdue sold only the eggs. After a few years, the company became a hatchery, selling laying chicks to other farmers. In the 1940s, he realized the real money was in selling broiler chicks. By the late 1960s, Perdue Farms, at that time run by Arthur's son, Frank, controlled everything from egg to table, getting into both the feed and processing parts of the chicken industry.

Over the next few decades, bolstered by a series of television ads touting his farm's production values and the marigold petals that made their chickens yellow, Frank's folksy face and the name Perdue became synonymous with chicken. Today, Frank's son Jim runs the company, appears in the company's commercials, and is responsible for Perdue's continual growth. The company launched a line of antibiotic-free chicken in the late 2000s and bought Coleman Natural Foods in 2011, making Perdue the nation's largest producer of USDA-certified organic chicken. While the organic lines account for only about 5 percent of Perdue's earnings, the demand is growing, which can only mean good things for Perdue's bottom line.

Chicken continues to be big business. In fact, over the last sixty years it has become the most popular meat in the United States. Chicken consumption has increased dramatically, going from twenty-eight pounds per capita

What Is a Chicken?

Of course, chickens themselves need no explanation. They're feathery flightless creatures that say, "bok bok," and taste mighty good fried or roasted. But can you fry a roaster or roast a fryer? What are "roasters" and "fryers" anyway?

Basically, these names refer to the size, and occasionally the age, of the chicken. Broilers and Fryers are both six to eight weeks old. The former weigh about 2½ pounds, the latter from 2½ to 3½ pounds. Roasters are much older, but still less than eight months old, and weigh from 3½ to 5 pounds. Then there are stewing chickens, a term that generally refers to old hens. And by old, we mean over ten months. They weigh from 5 to 7 pounds.

To make things more complicated, one can also buy capons, which are castrated 6- to 8-pound males, and non-castrated ones (roosters) that weigh the same but must be more than ten months old.

There's no stopping you from buying a roaster and cutting it into pieces and frying it, or from roasting a fryer chicken. It all depends on the amount of meat you need. Stewing chickens are tougher, so work best in situations where they are long cooked, or stewed. The same goes for roosters, which would be perfect for something like coq au vin. Capons tend to be fattier and more flavorful than other chickens, so are perfect for roasting. For the recipes in this book, unless otherwise indicated, fryer chickens are best if you plan to dissect a whole one. Otherwise, pre-packaged, pre-cut chicken parts of your choice are just dandy.

Parts

1 - Breast
2 - Drumstic / Leg
3 - Thig

4 - Wing
5 - Back
6 - Neck

© Thinkstock

in 1960 to a whopping eighty-three pounds in 2013. It's possible that this growth can be attributed to the country's concerns with fat and cholesterol, and the belief that eating chicken, particularly white meat, is a healthier choice than eating red meat. However, while the amount of beef, pork, veal, and lamb consumed in the United States within the same time-frame fluctuates a bit, it is only about thirty pounds less per capita in 2013 than in 1960. We just eat too much protein, but that's the subject for another book entirely.

The growth in our appetite for chicken has benefitted Maryland. According to the Delmarva Poultry Industry, Inc., the state's chicken production and processing accounts for 2,700 jobs and $133 million in wages, with a total economic impact of $1.3 billion. That's a lot of impact. However, while jobs and money are benefits of the chicken industry, there is a downside.

Chickens are animals. They eat, therefore they must poop. And they poop a lot; the Maryland Department of Agriculture says that the millions of chickens on Eastern Shore chicken farms produced 332,000 tons of manure in 2012. The good news: chicken manure is full of nitrogen, phosphorus, and potassium, all of which are essential for plant growth; hence, it makes great fertilizer. The bad news: it makes great fertilizer, full of nitrogen, phosphorus, and potassium. It might seem like a fine idea to spread the manure on surrounding croplands, but the amount of farmland on the Eastern Shore has diminished as the number of chickens (and chicken waste) has increased. Land has become over-fertilized, and the excess ends up as run-off, washed into the streams and rivers that flow into the Chesapeake Bay.

For those wondering why chicken farmers don't just process the manure much in the way municipalities treat human waste, the answer is simple: they can't afford to do that. While big corporations or integrators (as in "vertical integration") like Tyson and Perdue own the chickens, they do not raise them. Instead, they contract farmers to do it for them. According to a 2001 study by the National Contract Poultry Growers Association and the U.S. Department of Agriculture, the vast majority of farmers whose sole source of income comes from chickens live below the poverty line. That would make sense, as chicken is relatively inexpensive to the consumer. Big Chicken has to make a profit, so the farmers don't get much of a cut. They're also responsible for paying for the land on which they raise the chickens and the buildings in which they are raised, plus water, fuel, and labor. Essentially, the chicken farmers are paid for the services they provide, all stipulated by their contract with the integrator. They're also stuck with waste management.

Over the years, the chicken waste that has been repurposed in the most cost-efficient manner—fertilizer—has been a big part of the Chesapeake's problems. The phosphorus and nitrogen overload in chicken manure, when it finds its way into bodies of water, causes something called eutrophication. Basically, these elements act as fertilizer to algae. The excess algae growth blocks sunlight and the algae's decomposition reduces the amount of oxygen in the water, a condition known as hypoxia. Without sunlight and oxygen, both underwater grasses and the fish and shellfish they protect perish.

© Thinkstock

Thankfully, scientists realized some time ago that action was required to limit or possibly reverse the damage caused by over-nutrification. The feds instituted the Federal Water Pollution Control Amendments of 1972 to combat this problem along with other pollutants. While what we now call the Clean Water Act has been regulating the amount of pollution that comes from "point sources" like the chicken factories themselves, it had little impact on the problem caused by runoff of chicken waste used as fertilizer. In fact, "agricultural stormwater," as it's known, was exempt from the permitting requirements that controlled pollution limits for livestock facilities. In 2008, the U.S. Environmental Protection Agency (EPA) finally set requirements for land application of waste materials, however, requiring permits and setting limits does not eliminate the issue completely.

The problem with phosphorous pollution from chickens is seemingly unrelenting, but laws regulating the use of manure as fertilizer have grown stricter. Maryland has adopted a Phosphorus Management Tool (PMT) that will force farmers to use inorganic fertilizer if the levels of phosphorus in their soil are found to be too high. Farmers felt the new tool was punishment, as inorganic fertilizer is more expensive than the plentiful chicken manure they were already using. So what will happen with all the excess manure if fewer farmers will be able to use it? There are no hard and fast answers to that question, but things are being done. Both the State of Maryland and Perdue have been looking into ways to turn chicken manure into biofuel, examining proposals from various firms who want to build biomass boilers or anaerobic digester facilities on the Eastern Shore. On a less dramatic scale, there's a state Manure Matching Service that will pair farms with excess manure to farms in other parts of the state that need it and a Manure Transport Program that provides grants to help pay to move it around.

In the meantime, it doesn't look like the popularity of chicken is going to wane anytime soon. And why should it? Chicken is delicious. And while it's not as low in cholesterol when compared to red meat as people think (it's actually comparable), it is a bit lower in fat and calories. It's also versatile and relatively quick-cooking. Marylanders have their own special chicken dishes, too.

Maryland Fried Chicken

Fried chicken is one of those things that seems to have as many recipes as it has cooks. Maryland-centric cookbooks often have at least one recipe for Maryland fried chicken, and sometimes two or more. None of them are exactly alike, but what they seem to have in common is a cream gravy accompaniment. The differences between the recipes occur in the method of cooking. Some call for shallow frying; another technique requires steaming

© Kathy Wielech Patterson

the chicken after browning, to guarantee moist meat cooked through to the bone. In most recipes, the chicken is lightly dredged in seasoned flour, but there are one or two that involve a slightly more elaborate coating. We like the idea of frying-plus-steaming and a simple seasoning mix of salt and pepper and maybe a soupcon of Old Bay® Seasoning.

While a certain southern colonel's secret chicken recipe is popular worldwide, Maryland's own version is no slouch when it comes to fame. There are records of Maryland fried chicken showing up on restaurant menus the world over. Auguste Escoffier, the legendary chef who was instrumental in modernizing French cuisine in the early twentieth century, included a recipe for a dish called *poulet sauté Maryland* in his seminal 1903 *Le Guide Culinaire*.

Escoffier's dish is not exactly fried chicken with cream gravy. Instead, he advises cooks to pan fry bread crumb-coated chicken pieces and serve them with bacon, fried bananas, corn cakes, and a horseradish cream sauce. Bananas might not seem to be a particularly Maryland thing, but the port of Baltimore saw more than its fair share of them come through town in the late nineteenth and early twentieth centuries. Chicken à la Maryland became so popular it was even served as part of the first-class luncheon on the *R.M.S. Titanic* on April 14, 1912, the day before its fateful meeting with an iceberg.

Here's a classic version of the recipe, using the shallow fry and steam technique, and serving it with plain cream gravy. Don't take the cooking times as gospel. It may take a minute or two more or less to achieve browning. As long as the internal temperature of the chicken goes above 165°F (especially for dark meat) and the skin is browned and crisp, the dish is a success. Biscuits make a fine accompaniment. Or, if you are so inclined, corn firtters (see page 137), and fried bananas.

R.M.S. "TITANIC

APRIL 14, 1912.

LUNCHEON.

CONSOMMÉ FERMIER   COCKIE LEEKIE
FILLETS OF BRILL
EGG À L'ARGENTEUIL
CHICKEN À LA MARYLAND
CORNED BEEF, VEGETABLES, DUMPLINGS
FROM THE GRILL.
GRILLED MUTTON CHOPS
MASHED, FRIED & BAKED JACKET POTATOES
CUSTARD PUDDING   PASTRY
APPLE MERINGUE
BUFFET.
POTTED SHRIMPS
SALMON MAYONNAISE   SOUSED HERRINGS
NORWEGIAN ANCHOVIES
PLAIN & SMOKED SARDINES
ROAST BEEF
ROUND OF SPICED BEEF
VEAL & HAM PIE
VIRGINIA & CUMBERLAND HAM   BRAWN
BOLOGNA SAUSAGE
GALANTINE OF CHICKEN
CORNED OX TONGUE
BEETROOT   TOMATOES
LETTUCE
CHEESE.
CHESHIRE, STILTON, GORGONZOLA, EDAM,
CAMEMBERT, ROQUEFORT, ST. IVEL.
CHEDDAR

Iced draught Munich Lager Beer 3d. & 6d. a Tankard.

(SERVES 4–6)

1 cup flour

1 teaspoon salt

¼ teaspoon pepper

1 chicken, cut into 8 pieces

Fat for frying (lard or vegetable oil, or a combination of the two)

Unsalted butter

1 cup milk

Combine flour with salt and pepper and pour into a plastic zip-top bag. Place the chicken pieces in the bag, one at a time, and shake to coat with flour. Place coated pieces on a plate until each piece has made a trip through the flour. Reserve 2 tablespoons of the remaining flour.

Heat ¼ inch of fat in a large, heavy-bottomed, frying pan (a cast iron skillet is ideal) over medium-high heat. Put the chicken pieces in, skin side down. Cook for about 5 minutes, until the skin starts to brown, then turn each piece and cook for an additional 3 minutes. Turn the chicken over again, cover the pan most of the way, and allow the chicken to steam for 8 to 10 minutes. A meat thermometer stuck into the meatiest part of the chicken should read no less than 165°F. Remove the cover and cook an additional couple minutes on both sides if it hasn't browned to your liking.

Remove chicken from the pan and arrange on a platter. Remove all but 2 tablespoons of the fat from the pan. If there's not enough, add butter to make up the difference. Scrape up any browned bits stuck to the bottom. Stir in the 2 tablespoons of reserved seasoned flour and whisk until smooth. Gradually pour in the milk, whisking constantly. Cook until gravy is thick enough to coat the back of a spoon. Season with salt and pepper, if necessary.

Maryland Fried Chicken and Waffles with Maple Bacon Gravy

This more modern twist on Maryland fried chicken keeps the technique and cream gravy and adds bacon and maple, both of which scream for a crispy waffle accompaniment. (SERVES 4–8)

For chicken:

1 cup all-purpose flour

1 teaspoon Old Bay® Seasoning

Big pinch of salt

½ teaspoon freshly ground black pepper

8 skin-on, bone-in chicken thighs

Peanut oil for frying

For waffles:

1 cup yellow cornmeal, preferably stone ground

1 cup all-purpose flour

1 tablespoon baking powder

½ teaspoon salt

2 eggs

1½ cups (2 percent) milk

½ stick melted butter, cooled

For gravy:

Unsalted butter

2 tablespoons flour

2 cups rich chicken stock (preferably homemade)

2 slices cooked bacon, chopped

¼ cup heavy cream

2 tablespoons pure maple syrup

Salt and pepper

To serve:

2 tablespoons chopped scallions

To make chicken: Combine flour with Old Bay® Seasoning, salt, and pepper and place in a plastic zip-top bag. Place the chicken pieces in the bag, one at a time, and shake to coat with flour. Place coated pieces on a plate until each piece has made a trip through the flour. Reserve 2 tablespoons of the remaining flour.

Heat ¼ inch of fat in a large, heavy-bottomed, frying pan (a cast iron skillet is ideal) over medium-high heat. Put the chicken pieces in, skin side down. Cook for about 5 minutes, until the skin starts to brown, then turn each piece and cook for an additional 3 minutes. Turn the chicken over again, cover the pan most of the way, and allow the chicken to steam for 8 to 10 minutes. A meat thermometer stuck into the meatiest part of the chicken should read no less than 165°F. Remove the cover and cook an additional couple of minutes on both sides if it hasn't browned to your liking.

Remove chicken from the pan; drain on paper towel–lined plates.

To make waffles: Preheat waffle iron. Preheat oven to 250°F and place a baking sheet in the oven.

Combine cornmeal, flour, baking powder, and salt in a large bowl. In another bowl, beat the eggs, then whisk in the milk and butter until combined. Pour the wet ingredients into the dry and stir until combined.

Spoon batter into waffle iron according to manufacturer's directions. Cook until golden and crisp. Place cooked waffles onto the baking sheet in the oven. Repeat until all waffle batter is used.

To make gravy: Pour all but 2 tablespoons of fat out of the pan used to cook the chicken. Add butter to make up the difference, if needed. Whisk in flour. Cook for about 5 minutes, stirring regularly, to create a light blonde roux. Raise heat and whisk in chicken stock; bring to a boil. After a minute or two, when stock has thickened to gravy consistency, lower heat to medium and stir in the bacon, cream, and maple syrup. Season with salt and lots of freshly ground pepper to taste.

To serve: Stack two waffles on each plate, top with one or two pieces of chicken, and spoon over some of the gravy. Sprinkle with chopped scallions and serve.

© Thinkstock

Chicken Chesapeake

What exactly is chicken Chesapeake? We are hard pressed to answer that question. A dish bearing that name is seen on menus all over Maryland, and there are several recipes on the Internet, but it's difficult to find two that are exactly alike. There seems to be three general schools of thought in regard to the composition of chicken Chesapeake. Some folks cut a pocket into a boneless, skinless, chicken breast and stuff it with crab, like a Maryland version of chicken cordon bleu. Others top the chicken with a crab cake and serve it with or without a sauce of some sort. Still others incorporate the crab meat into a saucy topping for the chicken, like crab imperial or crab dip. There are versions that include thinly sliced cured ham, cream cheese, mushrooms and pasta, bacon and cheddar cheese, or all of the above. The only commonalities in all these dishes seem to be chicken and crab meat.

The earliest reference to a dish called "chicken Chesapeake" that we've seen was on a 1955 menu from the once-popular Chesapeake restaurant, in Baltimore. This version, chicken baked *en casserole* with broccoli and Mornay sauce, seems to be a variation of chicken Divan and is clearly named after the restaurant itself and not the origin of its ingredients.

So who was the first person to call a crab and chicken concoction "chicken Chesapeake?" And why crab and not oysters, or a combination of the two? These are questions that may never be answered, but it doesn't matter, as chicken and crab is a winning combination.

Chicken Chessie

COURTESY OF CHEF ANNMARIE LANGTON, GYPSY QUEEN CAFE

"I'm obsessed with Old Bay® Seasoning butter wings," says Chef Langton. And in this dish, she applies her obsession to a chicken leg stuffed with crab, putting a unique spin on a dish that doesn't have a clear classic version. If making a hollandaise sauce on the stove seems intimidating, use the blender technique on page 165, adding the corn, sugar, and parsley to the resulting sauce.
(MAKES 4–6 SERVINGS)

For the chicken:

1 can IPA-style beer (preferably Baltimore-produced Union Craft Double Duckpin)

1 cup apple cider vinegar

½ cup sugar

⅓ cup salt

2 garlic cloves, crushed

6–8 bone-in, skin-on chicken drumsticks

½ cup mayo

1 teaspoon lemon zest

2 teaspoons Worcestershire sauce

2 teaspoons yellow mustard

1 pound jumbo lump crabmeat, picked over for shells

Salt to taste

Olive oil

For the hollandaise:

4 egg yolks

2 tablespoons lemon juice

12 ounces unsalted butter, melted

1½ cups cooked corn kernels

1 teaspoon of sugar

1 teaspoon of fresh flat leaf parsley

For the Old Bay® Seasoning butter:

8 ounces unsalted butter

2 tablespoons Old Bay® Seasoning, or to taste

To serve:

3 ripe Maryland tomatoes, sliced thickly

To make the chicken: In a large plastic container with a lid, combine 3 cups of water with the beer, vinegar, sugar, salt, and garlic. Stir until the sugar and salt are dissolved. Refrigerate brine until cold, about 1 hour. Add the chicken. Cover container and refrigerate overnight.

The next day, remove the chicken from the brine and pat very dry with paper towels. Using your fingers, make a pocket by loosening the skin from the drumstick end of each leg in one piece. Do not tear the skin or completely detach it from the leg.

Preheat oven to 400°F.

Combine the mayo, lemon zest, Worcestershire, and mustard in a medium bowl. Mix well to combine. Gently fold in the crab meat. Season with salt to taste. If the mixture seems a bit dry, add a little more mayo.

Using a clean cutting board as a base, carefully stuff 2 tablespoons of the crab mixture under the skin of each leg. Use a large toothpick or small skewer to hold the skin in place over the crab. Set each stuffed drumstick skin-side-up on a lightly greased baking sheet. Brush each leg with a bit of olive oil.

Bake chicken for 30 to 35 minutes, or until the internal temperature is at least 165°F. If the chicken skin is not crisp at this time, put the chicken under the broiler for a few minutes.

To make hollandaise: If you have a double boiler, fill the bottom part halfway with water and bring to a boil. If you don't have one, fill a medium saucepan halfway with water and bring it to a boil. Turn temperature down so the water is at a bare simmer. In the top half of the double boiler (or a bowl big enough to fit on top of the pot comfortably so the bottom does not touch the water), whisk the eggs and lemon juice together vigorously until they are pale yellow. Do not let the eggs cook! Slowly dribble in the melted butter while whisking quickly until all of the butter has been emulsified into the eggs and sauce has doubled in volume. Remove the sauce from the heat and stir in the corn, sugar, and parsley. Keep warm over a bowl of barely simmering water until ready to use.

To make butter: Melt butter and stir in the Old Bay® Seasoning. Keep warm until ready to use.

Once chicken is done and crisp, give each leg a gentle toss in the butter sauce making sure the crab doesn't fall out.

To serve: Place two slices of tomato on each plate. Place a chicken leg or two on top of the tomatoes, drizzling with additional butter sauce. Pour the hollandaise in a puddle around the outside of the tomatoes.

Deviled Eggs with Smoked Trout and Crab

What came first, the chicken or the egg? Well, in this chapter, chicken recipes come first, but we can't ignore the best and most versatile part of the bird: the egg.

The word "deviled," culinarily speaking, ordinarily refers to the addition of mustard. If you use freshly picked (by you!) blue crab meat, you can double-devil the eggs by adding some of the crab's delicious greenish-to-brownish fat, known to Marylanders as "mustard." And while one doesn't necessarily think of trout and Chesapeake at the same time, there are several species of this fish in the Bay and its tributaries. If you don't have a local source for smoked trout and don't want to smoke your own (understandable!), Trader Joe's carries their own brand of canned smoked trout, in a convenient 3.9-ounce can just about perfect for this recipe. (MAKES 24)

12 large eggs

¼ cup mayonnaise

1 tablespoon extra virgin olive oil

1 teaspoon Dijon mustard

Crab mustard (optional)

½ teaspoon grated lemon peel

Pinch cayenne pepper

Salt and pepper to taste

4 ounces smoked trout, shredded

¼ cup crabmeat

Smoked paprika

Finely chopped chives

Put eggs in a large pot and cover with cold tap water. Bring to a boil. Turn off the heat, cover the pan, and allow the eggs to sit in the hot water for 15 minutes. Transfer eggs to a bowl of ice water and allow to cool completely. Peel under running water.

Dry eggs with a paper towel and cut in half lengthwise. Scoop the yolks into a medium bowl and smash with the back of a fork. Stir in the mayo, olive oil, Dijon, crab mustard (if using), and lemon peel until smooth and creamy, adding a bit more mayo if it seems too dry. Season yolks with cayenne and add salt and pepper to taste. Gently fold in the trout and crabmeat.

© Kathy Wielech Patterson

If you have a pastry bag with an extra-large coupling and round tip (like the ones used to frost cupcakes), use that. If not, spoon the filling into a plastic zip-top bag and snip a large enough opening into one corner so that the crab and trout pieces can flow easily. Pipe the eggs as decoratively as possible with the filling. Sprinkle a bit of the paprika and chives over each.

Serve at room temperature.

Roasted Tomato Clafoutis

Clafoutis, a French dish with lots of eggs and a bit of flour to keep it together, falls somewhere between a quiche and a custard. It puffs up like a soufflé while baking, then quickly deflates. A more familiar version of clafoutis is a dessert or breakfast dish made with cherries, but roasted mini heirloom tomatoes make it work as a savory course, too. (SERVES 8)

1 tablespoon extra virgin olive oil

2 cloves garlic, crushed

1 tablespoon chopped fresh rosemary

2 teaspoons light brown sugar

1½ teaspoon kosher salt (divided use)

1 pound cherry or grape tomatoes

1 tablespoon unsalted butter, at room temperature

1¼ cups milk

1 tablespoon sugar

6 eggs

¾ cup flour

2 tablespoons chopped fresh basil

Preheat oven to 350°F.

Combine oil, garlic, rosemary, brown sugar, and one teaspoon of kosher salt in a bowl. Add the tomatoes and toss to coat. Spread the mixture onto a foil-lined baking sheet and bake for about 45 minutes, until tomatoes are soft and starting to caramelize. Remove from the oven and allow to cool to room temperature.

Turn up oven temperature to 425°F.

Use the tablespoon of butter to grease a 10-inch cast iron skillet. Arrange the cooled tomatoes in the bottom, discarding any liquids that might be on the baking sheet.

© Kathy Wielech Patterson

Put the milk, sugar, eggs, and flour into a blender with ½ teaspoon of kosher salt and whiz to thoroughly combine. Stir in basil. Pour batter into prepared pan. Bake for 30 minutes, until puffed and browned. Allow to cool for 15 minutes before cutting into wedges.

Johnnycake Crab Benedict

COURTESY OF CHEF SCOTT HINES, B&O AMERICAN BRASSERIE

This twist on the classic eggs Benedict is all about Maryland products—corn, tomatoes, Old Bay® Seasoning, and blue crab. The Algonquin Indians of the Mid-Atlantic region are said to have taught the early colonists how to make johnnycakes, a corn flatbread used in place of the traditional English muffin. Fried green tomatoes add a bit of acid and crunch to this rich dish.
(SERVES 4)

For johnnycakes:

1 cup cornmeal

1 tablespoon sugar

1 teaspoon salt

1 cup boiling water

3 tablespoons milk

For fried green tomatoes:

1 cup flour

½ cup cornmeal

1 teaspoon salt

½ teaspoon pepper

1 cup buttermilk

2 green tomatoes, sliced ¼-inch thick

Oil for frying

For hollandaise sauce:

5 egg yolks

½ teaspoon cayenne pepper

2 teaspoons Old Bay® Seasoning

2 teaspoons fresh lemon juice

8 ounces unsalted butter, melted, kept warm

For the eggs:

1 teaspoon white vinegar

8 large eggs

To serve:

8 ounces lump crabmeat, picked over for shells

© Thinkstock

To make johnnycakes: Combine dry ingredients in a bowl. Pour boiling water over and stir to mix well. Stir in the milk. Spoon mixture onto a hot buttered griddle to form 3-inch pancakes. Cook on both sides until golden brown.

To make tomatoes: Place half the flour on a plate. Combine the remaining half of the flour with the cornmeal, season with salt and pepper, and place it on a separate plate. Put buttermilk in a bowl. Dip each slice of tomato first in the flour, then the buttermilk, then the cornmeal mixture. Place coated tomatoes on a plate and allow them to rest for a few minutes.

In a large frying pan or cast iron skillet, heat about ½ inch of oil. Fry tomatoes until crispy and golden brown on both sides. Remove from oil and drain on paper towel–lined plates.

To make hollandaise: Combine first four ingredients in a blender jar and blend for 45 seconds. Open the plastic lid on the blender and, while blender is running, slowly drizzle in the warm butter a few drops at a time. Blend until all butter is incorporated. If the sauce seems too thick, blend in tiny amounts of warm water until the desired consistency is achieved.

To make eggs: Put about 2 inches of water in a large saucepan and bring to a simmer. Add vinegar. Crack eggs into individual ramekins or small bowls and gently drop each of them into the simmering water. Space the eggs evenly in the water; depending on the size of your pan, you will need to cook them in batches of 2 to 4 eggs. Cook until the whites are firm but the yolks are still runny, 2 to 3 minutes. Remove eggs from pan with a slotted spoon and place onto a paper towel–lined plate until ready to use.

To serve: Place two johnnycakes on a serving plate. Top each with a slice of fried tomato and top with some of the crab meat. Place a poached egg on top of each and cover with hollandaise sauce.

Part 4
Restoration and Protection

For centuries, the Chesapeake watershed was viewed as a magical cornucopia, endlessly providing bounty that would maintain biological sustenance and economic growth. It's only been in the last fifty years or so that we've come to recognize how our exploitation of the water and the land is adversely affecting the Bay's ability to provide. Just as we had to face the limitations of building our existence around the finite resource of fossil fuels, we must reckon with the reality that, unless we find ways to manage the watershed in a responsible and sustainable manner, the bounty and our way of life will cease to exist.

Invaders of the Deep: Invasive Species

Man-made pollution isn't the only obstacle to keeping the flora and fauna of America's waterways healthy, there's also the matter of invasive species. Over the millennia, the Chesapeake Bay has evolved to be the perfect home for many varieties of fish, crustaceans, and grasses, which in turn have evolved to become the perfect inhabitants. These creatures need the Bay, and the Bay needs these creatures. When an alien species is introduced, be it accidentally or on purpose, that natural balance is disturbed.

From a February 20, 2008 article in *The New York Times*, "According to one estimate, invasive species in the United States cause major environmental damage and losses totaling about $137 billion per year." Many of these creatures are introduced to local estuaries via the ballast water of supertankers and cargo ships. Water, taken in through valves in the hull when these ships are at sea, is used to provide stability. With the water come small fish, shellfish, and pests like bacteria and jellyfish. When the ballast tanks are emptied, often into waters that may be thousands of miles away from where the ships set sail, these creatures are transferred. Sure, all bodies of water are rife with pests, but they are indigenous pests and essential parts of those particular ecosystems.

While ballast water will remain an issue until there are more regulations controlling the emptying and refilling of ballast tanks in coastal waters, sometimes the aliens are introduced on a much smaller scale. Which doesn't make them any less dangerous.

Snakeheads. Why Did It Have to Be Snakeheads?

In the early 2000s, there was a big brouhaha in the news about a non-native fish that had been found in a Maryland pond. The bloodthirsty beast had giant teeth, could breathe out of water, and was purported to walk on land. *National Geographic* dubbed it "Fishzilla," making it sound like the subject for a campy SyFy Channel movie. (And it was! Check out "Snakehead Terror," starring Bruce Boxleitner and Carol Alt.) The Northern Snakehead, as this particular species is commonly known, is as scary as reported, but not for the same reasons. These freshwater members of the *Channidae* family, with their large toothy mouths and slimy, snakeskin-patterned hides, can breathe air, thanks to something called a suprabranchial chamber that allows for oxygen absorption. But they do not walk. What they can do is wriggle short distances on their fins, and if kept moist these fish can stay

alive outside of water for a few days. However, they won't come charging out of the water to snatch small dogs or bite people on the ankles.

Northern Snakeheads, *Channa argus*, are a popular food in their native Asia. In China, they are boiled into a soup purported to have healing powers. In the past, live snakeheads were sold in Asian markets here in the United States but have been illegal to import since 2002. At that time, a reproducing population was discovered in a pond in Crofton, Maryland, in Anne Arundel County. A man who had purchased the fish to make a soothing tonic for a sick relative had released them when they were no longer needed, rather than doing the sensible thing and popping them into the freezer for later. The pond's population was exterminated, but by 2004, more snakeheads had found their way into the waters of the Potomac River and its tributaries and were busily feeding and breeding.

While snakeheads won't be stomping through your town causing mayhem and destruction any time soon, they are causing not-so-subtle changes to the ecosystem of the waters they inhabit. Voracious carnivores with no natural predators in the United States, these fish eat other fish, crustaceans, frogs, insects, even small birds and mammals. As they can live in a wide range of temperatures, with females laying up to 15,000 eggs at a time and one to five times per year, the potential for the species to expand and thrive elsewhere in the Chesapeake watershed is great.

The U.S. Fish and Wildlife Service and local Maryland, D.C., and Virginia agencies have been monitoring the Northern Snakehead in the Potomac through a tagging program. The fish have been found as far north as Carderock, Maryland (not far from Bethesda, in Montgomery County), and as far south as Machadoc Creek, in Virginia. Snakeheads have also been found in the Patuxent, Nanticoke, Wicomico, and Blackwater Rivers, and have popped up in ponds in Delaware and on the Eastern Shore. People catching *Channa argus* in Maryland or Virginia are required to kill the fish immediately by cutting off its head or gutting or filleting it. If it's a tagged fish, it's requested that it be reported to the U.S. Fish and Wildlife Service, and if it's found outside of the Potomac, it should be reported to the Maryland Department of Natural Resources as well.

So say you're a fisherman and you've just caught a 30-inch Northern Snakehead, lopped off the beast's head, and contacted the authorities. Now what do you do with it?

You eat it, of course.

Humans have done a real number on the oyster, crab, shad, and terrapin populations in the Chesapeake region simply by eating them. A Maryland summer just doesn't feel complete without feasting on steamed crabs at least once, twice, or even five (or more) times, and oysters on the half shell are a popular appetizer in all the months that have an "R" in them (and even in those without). While crabs are scarce and wild oysters are hard to come by, the numbers of shad and terrapin are so small that their harvest has been prohibited for many years. Snakehead, being a menace, has no fishing season and there are no catch limits. In fact, it's thought by some that were consumers to develop a taste for snakeheads, the creature could be eaten into extinction. Others, however, are concerned that the public may grow to like them a bit too much, and that desire might lead to demand and commercial fishing. Hey—it could happen. People actually eat tilapia on purpose now, and honestly, it doesn't even taste good.

Local chefs have been doing their part to encourage the public to eat snakehead. Chad Wells has been leading the battle cry in the Baltimore area. The Maryland native is a keen fisherman and likes to spend his free time away from his restaurant, Alewife, on his boat, catching dinner. He says the snakehead has been popping up more frequently these days, and definitely in places outside the Potomac. "Blackwater has snakehead now, and the Delaware and Susquehanna Rivers." And while gutting a snakehead definitely kills it, sometimes a busy fisherman doesn't have the ability to do that right then and there. "Take a pair of needlenose pliers and snip the gill plates," says Chef Wells, "they die instantly." That's also the advice given to participants in the annual Potomac Snakehead Tournament by Joe Love, Manager of the Maryland Department of Natural Resources Tidal Bass Program. After all, these fishermen are after the cash prizes given for heaviest fish, and gutting them reduces weight.

So what does a snakehead taste like? Very, very good. The meat is firm and moist, and doesn't toughen up as quickly as other meaty fish like tuna or salmon, so it's harder to overcook. The flavor is quite neutral, so it works in a number of preparation styles. Everything from fish and chips to barbecue snakehead *banh mi* sandwiches is a good use for this fish. But please, don't go liking them so much that they become a thing. We really do want them out of our waters.

Roses are Red My Love, Catfish are Blue

Snakeheads aren't the only non-native species causing problems in the Chesapeake. There are also blue and flathead catfish. While these fish don't have the scary made-for-TV-movie qualities of *Channa argus*—no giant teeth, size 11 feet, or appetite for small children—they are still a menace. Like snakeheads, both blue and flathead catfish are predators with a varied diet, the bulk of which includes fish like shad, river herring, menhaden, and our precious blue crabs. Even heron. And like snakeheads, they create high numbers of offspring. Both varieties of catfish can grow into behemoths weighing one hundred pounds or more. We don't mean to be shallow, but damn, they're ugly, too, what with their oddly smooth, scale-less bodies, fat heads, and those pervy little whiskers.

Unlike snakeheads, blue catfish, *Ictalurus furcatus,* weren't smuggled into the United States by enterprising Asian gourmets. They're native to Mississippi, Ohio, and Missouri, and can be found in Texas as well. Some smart person thought it would be a good idea to introduce them to Virginia for sport fishing purposes. Now they're eating their way through the Nanticoke, Patuxent, Choptank, Susquehanna, and Sassafras Rivers.

Blue catfish don't seem as much of a problem to the layman as other invasive species. "People think, 'oh, they're just catfish,'" says Chef Wells. "But the Bay's channel catfish don't get as big as a blue." So they don't need to eat as much. It's estimated that today, blue catfish outnumber native fish in some areas three to one, which is completely outrageous.

Flathead catfish, *Pylodictis olivaris,* is the closest relative to a fish called the Widemouth Blindcat, the only member of the genus Satan. (Yes, you read that right—there is a genus of fish called Satan.) While the Satanic Blindcats are endemic to Texas and haven't yet shown up in the Chesapeake Bay, its cousin Mr. Flathead is doing plenty enough damage on its own. The flatheads can grow to a length of sixty-one inches—that's five feet, one inch—and weigh as much as 123 pounds or about the size of a teenager. Thankfully, the average is closer to

© Kathy Wielech Patterson

a still-huge thirty inches. But they can live up to twenty-four years. And females can lay up to 1,200 eggs per pound of body weight. Thankfully, young flatheads can be cannibalistic, so not all of those baby fish will end up living to maturity. But entirely too many of them will.

Unlike some other catfish, which are bottom-dwelling scavengers, the flavors of the more predatorial blue and flathead catfish are mild and sweet. Like other flaky white fish, these catfish are versatile and can be used in a variety of ways. So, if you are able, please go catch and eat these fish. Often.

Pulling Mussels from the Shell

Besides the snakeheads and blue and flathead catfish, there are other non-native species to be concerned with. Creatures like the veined rapa whelk, likely a ballast-water import and currently found in the saltier waters of the Virginia end of the Chesapeake, are a threat to the Bay's oyster population. These sea snails, native to the Sea of Japan and East China Sea, were first discovered in Virginia in 1998. They can grow to six to seven inches, and possess heavy rounded shells with short spires that range in color from gray to reddish brown, usually with black veins going around the shell, dark brown dashes on the spiral ribs, and deep orange interiors. These prolific gastropods favor a diet of mollusks, like clams, mussels, and oysters. While they prefer saltwater, they can tolerate lower salinities, which makes them a potential threat to Maryland's portion of the Chesapeake.

You won't be finding rapa whelk on local menus anytime soon, but they've been called the "poor man's abalone," with a sweet and mildly briny flavor and a texture like a chewy clam.

Another of ballast water's contributions to the Chesapeake is the zebra mussel, *Dreissena polymorpha*. These tiny striped mollusks are usually the size of a fingernail but can grow to about two inches. Although small, these creatures are very efficient water filters, cleaning up to a liter of water per day. While, on the surface, these bivalves might seem beneficial in that they can clean the Bay much like an oyster does, it's actually too much of a good thing. Zebra mussels grow prolifically—females can lay over a million eggs per spawning season. So while cleaning the water, these large numbers of zebra mussels will consume much of the plankton that would normally feed the native species. Also, cleaner water allows more sunlight to penetrate, which causes plants growing on the riverbed to grow faster. When these plants decay, they wash up on beaches and cause other water quality issues.

© Thinkstock

The mussels also tend to hang out in massive clumps, which can encrust boat hulls, wreak havoc on power plant intake canals and boat motors, and infect water treatment plants. The U.S. Fish and Wildlife Service estimates that zebra mussels have inflicted billions of dollars of damage on both human and natural systems. And not just in the Chesapeake region. The International Union for Conservation of Nature (IUCN) has named *Dreissena polymorpha* one of the "100 of the World's Worst Invasive Alien Species." And here's the real kicker: they're not edible. Well, they're not *inedible*—birds will eat them—but they're so small as to not be worth the effort. On a good day, the edible portion of a typical black mussel is about as big as the tip of one's thumb. Consider that most zebra mussels, shell and all, are probably half that size; one would have to be pretty desperate to eat them. And apparently they're not particularly tasty, to boot. Additionally, since they are such good filters, the mollusks tend to accumulate toxins. It's believed that zebra mussels are the source of the avian botulism that has killed off thousands of birds, like cormorants and loons, in the Great Lakes area over the last decade.

So if we can't eat zebra mussels, how can we control them? Right now, that's a problem waiting for a good answer. Zebra mussels are susceptible to certain substances, like potassium chloride, which when applied to areas in quantity it can harm the mussels, but it is harmless to humans or wildlife. Another product, derived from a soil bacterium, has been found to be toxic to zebra mussels but safe for other species. Even so, a massive kill in an area as large as parts of the Chesapeake can have negative impacts. Large numbers of dying mussels will cause an increased demand for dissolved oxygen, which in turn will kill off aerobic bacteria, increasing populations of anaerobic bacteria, and accelerate algae growth. In other words, damned if you do, damned if you don't. The best thing that we can do right now is to prevent the spread of zebra mussels by practicing good boat hygiene—keeping vessels and equipment, including trailers, clean of mud, vegetation, and animal life; drying everything thoroughly, allowing for five days of drying time before entering new waters. Also, never introducing any fish, plants, or other wildlife to a body of water unless it came out of that same body of water. This is especially true of live bait—it should be disposed of in a trashcan and not in the water.

Yet another imported pest is the Chinese Mitten Crab, *Eriocheir sinensis*. Native to the Pacific coast of China and Korea, they are another one of the IUCN's one hundred worst invasive alien species. Also known as the Chinese river crab and the Shanghai crab, these creatures infested the San Francisco Bay area back in the 1980s. The Great Lakes were hit next, and now they've been found in the Chesapeake. The invasion started slowly; one male crab was spotted at the mouth of the Patapsco River in 2006 and in 2007, the first mature female was found near Kent Island.

Chinese mitten crabs are catadromous; they are born in saltwater, spend their adult lives in freshwater, then return to saltwater to spawn. According to the Invasive Species Specialist Group (ISSO), during mass migrations, these crabs contribute to the temporary local extinction of native invertebrates. It also causes erosion by burrowing and can cost fisheries money by consuming bait and trapped fish and also damaging gear. Fortunately, very few of them to date have been spotted in the Chesapeake. At any rate, the Chinese mitten crab is eminently edible, so if they do become an issue in the future, we can attempt to eat them into extinction.

Potomac Snakehead Tournament

What do you do when an invasive species is gobbling up all the indigenous creatures in the Potomac River and disrupting its fragile ecosystem? Put on a fishing contest where cash prizes are awarded to fishermen for catching as many of these critters as they possibly can. That's exactly the idea behind the Potomac Snakehead Tournament. Open to anyone with a Maryland or Virginia fishing license, the tournament allows sport fishermen who use a rod and reel or prefer to catch their prey with a bow and arrow to win prizes for hauling in the most snakeheads by weight or by catching the largest individual fish. Blue catfish are another dangerously invasive predatory fish that can weigh as much as fifty pounds, so there's also a special prize for the largest blue cat caught during the tournament.

The 2015 tournament began at Fort Smallwood State Park, in Charles County, Maryland, on the last Saturday in May. Teams of up to four fishermen stood in line to register. The parking lot was filled with trucks hauling boats of every style and design, from canoes to speedboats. Some participants with larger boats like cabin cruisers were already docked at the slips. Other boats—those owned by bow fishermen who have their best luck at night—were rigged with banks of halogen work lights aimed toward the water.

After registration, the rules were laid out by Joe Love from the Maryland Department of Natural Resources. The main rule is to bring the fish back dead. Since snakeheads can live for quite a while outside of water, it was important for the fishermen to pull out the gill arches either with pliers or, for the adventurous, with their hands, preferably while wearing heavy gloves. The participants had from 6 p.m. that evening to 10 a.m. the next morning to catch as many snakeheads as they could.

With the formalities out of the way, the fishermen dashed to their trucks and began a hurried (but orderly) race to the piers to unload their watercraft. Some had already mapped out their fishing spots and left the piers at full speed to reach these prime locations before anyone else. Others took a more leisurely approach, carefully searching the waters for snakeheads. Some of the bow fish-

ermen stayed out until after midnight while the rod-and-reel crowd headed back at sunset and set out again just before dawn the next day.

By noon on Sunday, a festival atmosphere had replaced the serious, competitive mood of the day before. A live band filled the air with bluegrass music, event sponsor Flying Dog Brewery provided free beer, and Chef Chad Wells from Alewife restaurant in Baltimore manned a grill, turning snakehead into tasty finger food. How does snakehead taste? Quite good actually, with a firm, meaty white flesh somewhat akin to mahi mahi. Chef Wells brought a Vietnamese flair to the fish by making *banh mi*-style snakehead sandwiches that disappeared almost as soon as he could plate them.

© Frances Burman

By 12:30 p.m., the real business got underway as the teams brought up their catches to be weighed. Out of the 127 teams registered, only about twenty-five actually had luck on the water and participated in the weigh-in. The bow fisherman fared the best: Team Shaft Assassins pulled in an amazing 230 pounds of snakehead. While Team Reel Finomenon came in third place with 153 pounds of snakehead, they also caught an award-winning blue catfish weighing in at thirty-eight pounds. The biggest individual snakehead, at fifteen pounds, belonged to Team RDC. In total, 239 northern snakeheads with a total weight of 1,745 pounds were caught, beating the previous year's record by 235 pounds.

The hope is that the snakehead population will drop to a point where the tournament will no longer be necessary. Josh Newhard of the U.S. Fish and Wildlife Service pointed out that the snakehead population in the Potomac has stabilized. However, he also noted that there are new instances of snakeheads popping up in areas outside of the Potomac, especially in areas along the Eastern Shore. It's possible that, in the future, events such as this may be needed in other parts of the state.

Grilled Snakehead with Fennel White Bean Ragout

COURTESY OF CHEF CHAD WELLS, ALEWIFE

Because it is so mild and meaty, snakehead takes well to pretty much any combination of flavors. You'll have leftover pesto, so use it on pasta later in the week.
(MAKES 6 SERVINGS)

To make the ragout:

3 fennel bulbs

¼ cup diced onion

2 tablespoons blended oil

1 cup cherry tomatoes, sliced

6 cloves garlic, minced

1 tablespoon dry oregano

Juice of 1 lemon

2 tablespoons tomato paste

3 tablespoons vegetable broth

3 tablespoons tomato juice

1 (15-ounce) can cannellini beans, drained and rinsed

To make the sundried tomato pesto:

2 cups sundried tomatoes

¼ cup shredded Parmesan cheese

¼ cup packed fresh basil leaves

¼ cup packed fresh parsley leaves

2 cloves garlic

1 tablespoon kosher salt

2 teaspoons lemon juice

1½ cups extra virgin olive oil

To make the fish and to serve:

6 (8-ounce) portions of snakehead

Salt and freshly ground black pepper

1 lemon

To make ragout: Trim bottoms of fennel bulbs. Reserve stalks and feathery fronds and set aside. Cut fennel bulbs in half and make a v-shaped cut to remove the cores. Slice the rest of the fennel thinly. Thinly slice some of the reserved stalks and fronds to equal 1 cup.

Put sliced fennel and stalks in a saute pan with onion and oil. Sweat vegetables until they start to soften. Add cherry tomatoes and garlic. Add reserved fronds and oregano and cook, stirring occasionally, until fennel is tender. In a small bowl, stir together lemon juice, tomato paste, vegetable broth, and tomato juice until well combined, then add to pan of fennel. Cook until liquid has thickened, then stir in beans and cook until heated through.

To make the pesto: Process all ingredients in a food processor to a paste with a bit of texture.

To make the fish: Lightly season fillets with salt and pepper on both sides. Cook on a hot grill or grill pan for about 4 minutes per side.

To serve: Place a bed of the fennel ragout in the middle of a plate. Top with a portion of the fish and give it a squeeze of lemon juice. Add a dollop of the pesto to the top of the fish.

Southwest Snakehead and Potato Cakes with Avocado Dill Purée and Corn Salad

COURTESY OF CHEF CHAD WELLS, ALEWIFE

Coddies are a somewhat old-fashioned food item that can still be found here and there in Baltimore City. Made primarily with seasoned mashed potato and occasionally some actual fish, they are enjoyed with mustard and saltines. Chad Wells has taken the concept of the coddie and turned it into something much grander, and he uses plenty of fish in them, too. Rather than crackers, he serves his fish cakes with a crispy corn salad and an avocado puree flavored unexpectedly with dill.

(MAKES 8 SERVINGS)

For the cakes:

3 eggs, lightly beaten

¼ cup mayonnaise

2½ tablespoons chipotle purée

1½ teaspoons ground cumin

10 chives, minced

1 tablespoon garlic powder

1 tablespoon minced cilantro

1 teaspoon fresh lime juice

¾ pound cooked snakehead meat, flaked

2 cups mashed potatoes

1 cup cooked black beans

Up to 4 cups bread crumbs

Blended oil for frying

Cornstarch

All-purpose flour

Paprika

Salt and pepper

For the purée:

2 avocados

1 ounce chopped dill, stems removed,

1 tablespoon kosher salt

¾ cup crème fraîche

2 teaspoons honey

1½ teaspoons lime juice

1½ teaspoons cider vinegar

For the corn salad:

2 ounces bacon, diced

½ red pepper, diced

1 jalapeno pepper, diced

½ red onion, diced

2 cups corn kernels

Juice of 1 lime, or to taste

Kosher salt

To make cakes: In a bowl, stir together the eggs, mayo, chipotle purée, cumin, chives, garlic powder, cilantro, and lime. In another bowl, combine the fish, potatoes, and black beans. Pour in the mayonnaise mixture and stir well to combine. Add as much of the bread crumbs as needed to form firm cakes (firmer than crab cakes).

Once the mixture is homogeneous, cover the bowl and refrigerate for 2 hours.

When ready to cook, heat the oil in a large saute pan. Form three 4-ounce cakes with the fish mixture. Dredge each in a coating made from three parts cornstarch to one part flour, seasoned with a bit of paprika, salt and pepper. Fry cakes on both sides until crispy and golden brown. Drain on paper towel–lined plates.

For the puree: Scoop the flesh of the avocados into a food processor. Add the remaining ingredients and pulse to a purée. Transfer to a bowl; cover and chill until ready to use.

For the salad: Cook the bacon over medium heat until fat starts to render and bacon begins to brown. Add the peppers, onion, and corn, and cook until bacon is done but vegetables are still crisp. Season with lime juice and kosher salt.

To serve: Dollop the avocado puree on a plate, top with some of the crab salad. Stack two of the snakehead cakes on top.

Blackened Blue Catfish with Cheese Grits and Greens

COURTESY OF CHEF CHAD WELLS, ALEWIFE

Chef Wells says the blackening seasoning works well on pretty much any meat or seafood item. This recipe makes more than you'll need for the catfish, so keep the rest in a jar on your spice rack. And if you can get Palmyra cheddar, made in Hagerstown, Maryland, then use it. If not, any cheese will do.
(MAKES 6 SERVINGS)

For blackening seasoning:
6 tablespoons garlic powder
6 tablespoons kosher salt
5 tablespoons brown sugar
5 tablespoons sweet paprika
3 tablespoons ground coriander
3 tablespoons ground cumin
2 tablespoons ground cinnamon

For greens:
1 onion, diced
½ pound bacon, diced
2 pounds collard greens

2 quarts chicken stock
2 cups apple cider vinegar
Salt

For grits:
2 cups white grits, preferably Anson Mills
3 cups chicken stock
2 tablespoons heavy cream
2 tablespoons shredded cheddar cheese
Salt and pepper to taste

For fish:
6 (8-ounce) portions blue catfish fillets
Blended oil

To make seasoning: Combine all ingredients in a bowl. Pour into a container with a lid, like an empty spice jar.

To make the greens: Cook the onions and bacon together in a large pot until onion begins to soften. While they're cooking, wash the greens thoroughly. Remove the stems and chop the leaves.

When the onions are softened, add the greens. Cook, stirring often, until greens appear sweaty. Add the chicken stock and vinegar and bring to a boil. Turn heat to a simmer and cook for 2 hours, until greens are very tender. Add salt to taste.

To make grits: Simmer the grits in the stock until grits are tender. Stir in the heavy cream and the cheese. Season with salt and pepper to taste. Keep warm.

To make the fish: Pat the catfish fillets dry with paper towels. Encrust both sides heavily with the blackening seasoning.

Heat a cast iron skillet until screaming hot and add a couple tablespoons of the oil. Add the fish to the pan, pressing lightly on the fillets with a spatula to ensure the entire piece of fish gets an even sear. Cook for a few minutes, then try to slide the spatula under the fish. If it gives any indication of sticking, wait a bit longer. Once the fish is fully cooked on the first side, it will be easy to flip. Do the same for the second side.

Serve fish with some of the grits and some of the greens.

The Jewel in Maryland's Crown:
Techniques for Preserving the Bay

There's a telling phrase on the Chesapeake Bay Foundation's website: "At its healthiest in the early 1600s . . . " In other words, the Bay watershed was in optimal condition back before the first gaggles of Europeans staggered off whatever sailing vessels they arrived on and settled these shores. That is, of course, assuming that the Native Americans here before them hadn't already caused damage, which is probably safe to say. Remember that the beginnings of the Chesapeake date from the late Pleistocene era, about 18,000 years ago—small potatoes in the scheme of the estimated 4.5 billion or so years that this blue planet has been hanging around our solar system. Yet in a mere four centuries, about one forty-fifth of the time that what we know as the Chesapeake Bay drainage region has existed, we have managed to eat several species into near-extinction, seriously deplete the numbers of other fish and mollusks, and pollute the waters with everything from hazardous chemicals to what are charitably called "nutrients," but that certainly aren't vitamin-fortifying the Bay in any positive way.

The Chesapeake Bay Foundation (CBF) published a health index in 2014 that rated the Bay at 32 out of 100 points. Bad, but not quite as bad as in 2008, when the Chesapeake scored 28/100. The *State of the Bay Report*, released every two years, measures thirteen indicators of the Bay's health, including numbers of various fauna, the health of the land and flora including underwater grasses, and things like water clarity, toxics, dissolved oxygen, and those pesky nutrients, namely nitrogen and phosphorus. Each indicator is assigned a score between 1 and 100 and a letter grade. The 2014 report noted that ten indicators either improved or stayed the same, while three fell. Sounds good, but a score of 32 is far below the goal of 70, and we'll never see the 100-point score that the Bay would have earned back in the 1600s. Despite the low numerical score, the overall letter grade isn't the expected F (written in red pen and circled), but somewhere closer to D-plus.

The last *State of the Bay Report*, from 2012, demonstrated that rockfish and crabs were doing pretty well. Only two years later, however, we see both earning lower scores. There has been a rockfish population decline since 2003, triggering conservation action and cutbacks in catch allowances starting in 2015. The blue crab population dropped dramatically, to less than half of the 2012 level. There are far fewer spawning female crabs, and the numbers of juvenile crabs to reach maturity were lower than expected. Oysters, which scored an F in 2012, are on the comeback trail, due largely in

© Jay Fleming

part to the intense restoration efforts that plant a billion or so baby oysters per year. Nearly one million bushels were harvested Bay-wide during the 2013–2014 season, the best numbers since 1987. Shad are unchanged, still earning a big fat F.

There's also the matter of climate change. Despite the unbelievers, the average temperature in the Chesapeake has gone up two degrees since the 1930s. While that might seem like a small increase, warmer waters hold less dissolved oxygen than colder waters. The 2014 *State of the Bay Report* showed an increase in dissolved oxygen in the Chesapeake—an increase of twelve points over 2012—and a smaller dead zone, but if you recall, that particular summer was cooler than normal. By the end of that summer, the dead zone, largely a result of nitrogen and phosphorus pollution, was back to "above average" size. This shows that seemingly small changes can make a significant impact on the health of the Bay.

Overall, it's a report card that would disappoint any good parent. Unfortunately, in the Chesapeake's case, we can't send polluters to their rooms or revoke their video game privileges. What we can do is to continue to work diligently to fix the many problems the Bay faces using all of the resources available, many of which involve legislation.

Save the Bay

In a perfect world, people do the right thing. Laws are created and upheld. Things work, and everyone is happy. If a perfect world existed, the Chesapeake Clean Water Blueprint could be the solution to the Chesapeake Bay's problems. The Blueprint has three major components: it sets two-year progress milestones; puts responsibility on everyone; and imposes consequences on failure.

In this case, the "everyone," includes the six states (Maryland, Delaware, Virginia, Pennsylvania, West Virginia, New York) and the District of Columbia that make up the Chesapeake Bay Watershed. Back in 1972, provision 303(d) of the Federal Water Pollution Control Act, more commonly known as the Clean Water Act, mandated that all states create a list of impaired waters and develop a Total Maximum Daily Load. The TMDL is an estimate of the maximum amount of pollution a body of water can accommodate and still meet quality standards. While the TMDL was a requirement, the EPA didn't enforce anything until nearly forty years later with the establishment of the Chesapeake Clean Water Blueprint in 2010. At that time, the seven jurisdictions had to develop Watershed Implementation Plans (WIPs)—and implement them—in order to meet a new federal TMDL for the Bay by 2025.

In a perfect world, there wouldn't be money problems, misinformation, or corporate lobbyists. Because for every person in this non-perfect world looking toward the future, hoping for a clean Chesapeake that will continue to provide habitat for wildlife, nourishment for the masses, and a modest income for those who fish and farm the lands nearby, there is at least one who is more concerned about what the Bay can do for them right now, another person who thinks that taking measures to save the Chesapeake will be too costly, and still another who doesn't know or doesn't care.

The watermen and farmers of the Chesapeake region are a major component in plans to keep the Bay healthy. For generations, they have reaped the benefit of the vast amounts and varieties of edible shell- and fin-fish in the Chesapeake. These days, however, with the numbers of rockfish and crabs yet again declining, and the general health of the waters falling into

the "not so hot" category, not only are these species suffering, but so, too, are the livelihoods of the men and women who work the Bay and its tributaries. It's completely understandable that they don't want new regulation on what they can catch and how much, and where they can and cannot fish. If they can't do their jobs, they can't put food on the table. But Bay restoration is very much a "big picture" issue. Just because the things that are being done to restore the Chesapeake might be inconvenient for some, that doesn't mean they shouldn't be done, and the sooner the better.

Fortunately, the federal government is on board. On May 12, 2009, President Barack Obama issued Executive Order 13508 on Chesapeake Bay Protection and Restoration. This was viewed as a "big step forward" by the Chesapeake Bay Foundation. In this groundbreaking strategy, the President recognizes the Chesapeake for the "national treasure" that it is, and takes some of the onus for the Bay's restoration into the hands of the federal government. The fed, after all, is one of the biggest landowners in the watershed, owning 5.3 percent of it, including military installations, parks, and monuments, so it's in their best interest to lead by example in keeping the area healthy.

The order establishes a Federal Leadership Committee (FLC) for the Chesapeake Bay, chaired by the Administrator of the EPA, with reps from departments of Agriculture, Commerce, Defense, Homeland Security, Interior, and Transportation. These heavy hitters are collaborating with the state and local agencies, businesses, and individuals who have been working to protect the Chesapeake for decades now.

Maryland is so far on track to meet some of the 2017 targets of the Chesapeake Clean Water Blueprint, namely those for phosphorus and sediment from sewage plants and agriculture. Nitrogen targets are still a ways away, as is a reduction in urban runoff. But we can't and shouldn't just let the government take over and save the Chesapeake. There are things that all of us—farmers, factory owners, fishermen, and city dwellers—can do to play our part.

Gray Skies Frowning at Me

While there's a great deal of focus placed on pollution that is either dumped directly into the Bay or placed there indirectly through run-off, pollution can also attack by air. Just as we have a Chesapeake watershed, there's a Chesapeake airshed that is nine times larger (approximately 570,000 square miles) stretching to include the state of Ohio and parts of Indiana, Michigan, Tennessee, Kentucky, and North Carolina. Airborne pollutants are pumped into the air by stationary sources like power plants and factories, by mobile sources like cars and planes, and by natural sources like livestock and poultry. In fact, one of the major airborne pollutants that threatens the Bay is the ammonia released from farm animals' manure and urine. About one-third of the nitrogen reaching the Bay comes from ammonia, with the remaining two-thirds coming from the burning of fossil fuels. Fossil fuels also contribute polycyclic aromatic hydrocarbons (PAHs), substances that have been found to be carcinogenic.

These airborne pollutants, along with mercury and myriad other chemicals, eventually float down to the water's surface or are flushed out of the sky in the form of rain. They are then absorbed by the fish and plant life, causing disease and other imbalances in the ecosystem.

While ammonia output from agricultural activities shows no sign of abating, state and federal regulations have helped to reduce some of the emissions from mobile and stationary sources. As of this writing, a smog prevention bill is working its way through the Maryland legislature. The Clean Power Plan, another Obama-led federal initiative, is designed to cut back the amount of greenhouse gases, which include nitrogen oxides, emitted from power plants. As we know, adding nitrogen to the water exacerbates the already imposing problem of algae blooms and dead zones fed by over-nutrification. The EPA believes the Clean Power Plan can produce a 72 percent reduction in nitrogen emissions. Every little bit helps.

Given the immense size of the airshed, simply controlling the pollution in Maryland and in the surrounding states is not enough. The Bay must rely on the kindness of the nation in battling air pollution. More grass roots efforts like driving low-emission vehicles, using alternative fuels, and planting more trees must be expanded to help not just the Bay, but the nationwide air pollution problem. Trees capture airborne pollution and absorb it into their leaves and root systems before it can reach the ground. Forests can capture 85 percent of airborne nitrogen. The more trees we have, the less nitrogen can reach the Bay.

Raindrops Keep Fallin' On My Roof

There are also some relatively smaller things being done that, in the long run, can make a difference. One of those is the so-called "rain tax," for which former Maryland Governor Martin O'Malley took a lot of flak. Much of the public disdain for the policy came from the usual suspects: Ms Understanding and Ms Information. For instance, in 2014, nearly two years after the bill was passed, *Forbes Magazine* published a poorly researched opinion that claimed, "Maryland is the only state in the country that taxes the amount of rain that falls." Not only is the tax not on the rain itself, but stormwater fees have been in place in different parts of the country since Washington State instituted such a fee in 1974. Since then, many hundreds of communities in thirty-nine states and Washington D.C. have implemented fee-funded stormwater utilities. In Maryland, only the ten most populous jurisdictions—Anne Arundel, Baltimore, Carroll, Charles, Frederick, Harford, Howard, Montgomery, and Prince George's Counties, and Baltimore City—are subject to stormwater fees.

If you're a city homeowner, you may have occasionally taken a hose to your front walk to give it a bath on a hot summer day. In doing so, you've seen the filth that washes off the sidewalk into the gutter. Similarly, every time it rains on a hard surface like a sidewalk, road, or roof, pollutants are washed into nearby streams and rivers. Some of it is residue from burning fossil fuels, some are invisible pollutants like bacteria, and in populous areas it might be actual trash, like the fast food wrappers some don't think twice about dropping on the ground instead of disposing of them properly. You can consider this type of pollution the urban counterpart to the agricultural stormwater that washes excess fertilizer nutrients into streams and rivers, and, ultimately, the Bay. City dwellers and suburbanites are just as responsible for water pollution as corporations and farmers.

Frustrated with the fact that states in the watershed were not reaching their goals for cleaning up the Bay as prescribed by the Chesapeake Clean Water Blueprint, the Chesapeake Bay Foundation and other plaintiffs threatened to sue the EPA. To avoid the lawsuit, a settlement was reached that applied real consequences for states that did not reach the clean-up mandates. In response, the Maryland legislature enacted a stormwater fee to raise the additional revenue needed for the clean-up efforts. At the time, it was colloquially referred to as a "user fee" on residential properties.

To control this type of run-off pollution, utilities must be set up to slow down and filter pollutants. For instance, most storm drains dump stormwater directly into rivers and streams, unfiltered and untreated. A stormwater fee provides dedicated revenue that enables jurisdictions to install stormwater management practices, which will help the state meet its TMDL.

In April of 2015, Maryland Governor Larry Hogan allegedly repealed the "rain tax," although this was just spin. Hogan's repeal was rejected. Instead, a new measure—introduced by Maryland Senate President Thomas V. Mike Miller Jr.—known as SB 863, Rain Tax Mandate Repeal (Watershed Protection and Restoration Programs, Revision), passed one vote shy of unanimously. Rather than repeal the fee entirely, the mandate was removed. This allows jurisdictions flexibility in complying with federal stormwater management requirements, such as offering exemptions to veterans' groups. Some will continue employing the fee; some will find other monies, such as designating a portion of property taxes to fund stormwater projects. In any case, the same jurisdictions continue to share the very expensive responsibility of financing stormwater remediation in order to meet Maryland's TMDL.

Farm Aid

Agricultural stormwater and soil erosion mean that the bucolic green fields of corn, soybeans, and other produce that cover swaths of the Chesapeake Bay Watershed are one of the major sources of the Bay's pollution problems, and farmers are required to participate in conservation efforts by employing Best Management Practices (BMPs). There are five priority practices that can reduce the amount of nitrogen flowing into the Bay by more than half. These include streamside fencing and buffers, cover crops, conservation tillage, and nutrient management plans (NMPs).

In 2013, the Maryland General Assembly passed SB1029, the "Maryland Agricultural Certainty Program." With this program, farmers who voluntarily meet 2025 water-quality goals today are offered flexibility in meeting the goals of new laws and regulations. The program creates an incentive to meet the state's goals for the TMDL. The new legislation makes sure farmers are implementing a Soil Conservation and Water Quality Plan along with a current Nutrient Management Plan to address the TMDL. Currently, it seems that the vast majority of Maryland farms are well on their way to meeting the 2017 TMDL goals for both nitrogen and phosphorus reduction and have surpassed the sediment reduction goal.

Chicken Shit Is Not a Penny-Ante Problem

The nearly one-third billion chickens raised on the Eastern Shore every year aren't themselves so much the problem. Not individually, anyway, since we eat most of them before they're more than a couple months old. But the amount of waste they produce, collectively, is monumental, and therein lies the biggest problem: Where do we put the mountains of poop?

Traditionally, chicken manure has been used as fertilizer. It's loaded with nutrients like phosphorus and nitrogen which are great for soil. But not so great for the flora and fauna of the Chesapeake Bay, where a good portion of it ends up. For years there have been regulations on the amount of pollution that comes directly from livestock facilities, like chicken factories, but nothing was done at all about controlling what is known as "agricultural stormwater." So while a chicken farmer couldn't back a truck full of manure up to the Choptank River and dump it directly into the water, he could let the farmer next door use his manure to fertilize his farmland. Mother Nature, in the form of rain, would take care of the polluting part. And as we all know, she's rather hard to control.

An EPA report from 2011 stated that excess nutrients are "associated with many large-scale environmental concerns, including eutrophication of surface waters, toxic algae blooms, hypoxia, acid rain, nitrogen saturation in forests, and global warming." In 2008, the EPA set requirements for the land application of waste materials, involving permits and such, but that didn't solve the problem by a long shot. In 2010, former Maryland Governor Martin O'Malley acknowledged that the tool farmers were using to determine whether or not their soil needed phosphorus was outdated. His proposal for a new Phosphorus Management Tool (PMT) was applauded by conservation groups but jeered by farmers who thought the tool would be too costly and "unnecessary." The new PMT wasn't close to becoming reality until the end of 2014, at which time O'Malley was leaving his role in Annapolis to chase other, larger, political aspirations.

A Salisbury University economic impact study on the PMT, commissioned by the Maryland Department of Agriculture, projected large financial losses for Maryland's farmers. Current Governor Larry Hogan appeared to take the farmers' side, at first claiming he would "pull the plug" on the project, vowing to come up with a better way to deal with the Bay's pollution. While Hogan did put the kibosh on O'Malley's plan, he didn't decimate it entirely, either. After all, the EPA needed something to be done about nutrient run-off, and done now.

Hogan's new plan, the Agriculture Phosphorus Initiative, is still quite aggressive. According to Maryland Agriculture Secretary Joseph Bartenfelder, the initiative makes "only four significant enhancements" to the old plan. The first is to make sure farmers have enough time to understand the new requirements, adding a full year to the implementation schedule. However, in a measure more strict than the original plan, farms with a soil Fertility Index Value (FIV) of 500 or greater are immediately banned from applying fertilizer containing additional phosphorus. It's been estimated that this affects about 20 percent of the farms on the lower Eastern Shore. Additionally, every farm that meets certain economic and animal weight standards must submit and follow a nutrient management plan. These farms will undergo testing every six years, giving the state an idea of where the nutrient-rich soil that can no longer be administered on shore lands can be used instead. Finally, solid plans must be developed for alternate uses or relocation of excess manure, as in working out ways of getting the manure from the shore to those nutrient-needy farms elsewhere in the state.

Fishing Around

Besides tidying up after ourselves to keep the waters of the Chesapeake clean and habitable, we also need to take steps to promote the various flora and fauna that live in the Bay. This includes the creatures that have sustained, those fortunate enough to have lived in the state of Maryland over many generations. We can only hope that someday a cleaner Chesapeake will be once again teeming with crabs, oysters, and rockfish so that our children and our children's children can also enjoy these delicious things.

Oyster Restoration

We have a much better chance of restoring the Bay's oyster population than any other. Oysters are perhaps the most beneficial to water quality, so they are a fine thing on which to focus. There are any number of organizations devoted to studying the problem of the Chesapeake's depleted oyster population. Maryland Sea Grant has supported a variety of research, education, and public-outreach projects. The Oyster Restoration Workgroup helps states along the eastern seaboard to "address questions related to shellfish restoration success, especially all pertinent issues associated with the restoration of both intertidal and subtidal oyster reefs." Assembling, collating, and analyzing volumes of data related to oyster restoration initiatives is the job of the Oyster Restoration Evaluation Team. They assist the

numerous organizations involved with understanding the collective goals and how successful these organizations were in reaching those goals.

On a more grassroots level, the Oyster Recovery Partnership (ORP) has several projects in the works to not only rebuild the oyster population but raise awareness of the issue in the community. Since oysters like to nest on top of beds of oyster shells, the ORP has collected hundreds of thousands of oyster shells from area restaurants and seafood distributors to create new beds. Three trucks make regular visits to pick up shell from restaurants and commercial processing houses in Maryland, Delaware, Washington D.C., and Northern Virginia and deliver it to their facility in Cambridge, which is about as large as the Baltimore Ravens' football stadium. The shell sits in the open air for a year, allowing the sun and flies to do much of the cleaning naturally. Then the shell is washed in giant machines with river water and allowed to remain in setting tanks filled with river water. As the shell sits, oyster larvae are introduced to the surface of the shell. This larvae-encrusted shell is then taken out in the bay on workboats and dumped into the water onto reefs.

In 2015, in cooperation with the University of Maryland Center for Environmental Sciences (UMCES) Horn Point Laboratory, the ORP placed 535 million spat on these shell beds in the Chesapeake Bay. In addition to using public waters, the Maryland Grow Oysters (MGO) program is a joint effort with the Maryland Department of Natural Resources (DNR), UMCES Horn Point, and other groups to get waterfront property owners to grow oysters in cages suspended from their private piers. The program started in the Tred Avon River with a few hundred cages, and has since expanded to thirty creeks and rivers with 8,000 cages.

In just a few short years, aquaculture has raised the numbers of oysters in the Chesapeake. While cultured oysters are meant for human consumption, and most of those are triploids, which do not spawn, their mere physical presence in the Bay and its tributaries has increased the water quality in those areas. With the increased water clarity we see underwater grasses—an essential component of a healthy Bay—thriving and creating habitat for other filter-feeding organisms as well as crabs and fish.

While aquaculture provides answers for human consumption and environmental cleanup, it's the replenishment of wild oyster populations that will help the economic question for watermen and commercial processing houses. Unfortunately, healthy restoration involves placing many oyster reefs off-limits to watermen. The O'Malley administration took away 25 percent of the oyster reefs for sanctuaries in addition to more reefs for aquaculture. Harris Creek, for example, has 370 acres of protected reef restoration with vast quantities of larvae floating out of Harris Creek into the rest of the bay and flushing back into the Choptank River. While this is a remarkable biological success, it does little to help the watermen who can't harvest any of those oysters. The Hogan administration is considering rotational harvesting to relieve the issue. There are many variations on this fishery technique, but by closing some areas for a few years and opening up other areas for a few years, it is possible for oyster restoration to proceed while still providing watermen with an opportunity to make a living. To this end, the large-scale oyster restoration project for the Tred Avon River has been halted as of early 2016.

Crab Restoration

There are, so far, not that many specific things that we can do to help the Maryland blue crab. We can, of course, manage the numbers that are caught in a given season, and put restrictions on catching smaller crabs. This has worked well enough that there isn't a steady annual decline in the crab population, but not well enough that there's been a boom in the opposite direction, either.

Restoring the crab population is one of those things that will hopefully come when the rest of the Bay is in better health. When there are fewer dead zones, more dissolved oxygen in the water, and a continued improvement in the amount of underwater grasses that provide habitat, more crabs can thrive. There are also things that we can do, you and I, to help the crabs—and the rest of the Bay's inhabitants. They simply involve reducing pollution of all kinds. Drive less. Don't fertilize your lawn. Make sure to pick up after your pets. And, if you own land, plant bushes and trees to increase oxygen in the air. You can also plant something called a "rain garden." It's essentially a large bowl of plants that directs stormwater into the ground rather than allowing it to flow across impermeable surfaces and pick up pollutants on the way to the storm drain. Rain gardens have specific requirements that can be found online at www.bluewaterbaltimore.com. Some folks may qualify for a financial incentive, which always makes everything more attractive.

There's also the matter of crab aquaculture. While Maryland doesn't seem to be able to come up with the funds to create a large-scale crab hatchery, the Gulf Coast Marine Life Center has. And they are working with the University of Maryland Institute of Marine and Environmental Technology's Aquaculture Research Center (ARC) to take a dozen-plus years of research on culturing crabs to potentially repopulate the Chesapeake and use it instead to enhance the numbers of crabs in the Gulf of Mexico. We will cynically note that, while this program does nothing for the Chesapeake itself, it will be useful to the consumer, as we have come to rely on imported Gulf crabs to fill our bellies for years now.

We can hope that the Gulf project is a roaring success and that both federal and state legislators will see that making the investment (in something largely possible because of Maryland's own scientists) is a prudent thing to do for the Chesapeake Bay.

Fish Restoration

As with crabs, the best way to restore the various populations of fish in the Bay is to enforce moratoriums against fishing particular species, and limiting the catches of others. It might be suggested to recreational fishermen that they return everything they catch back to the water. But this only addresses the problem of overfishing. A bigger problem that is much harder to control is the damage that invasive species are creating. Voracious carnivores like the northern snakehead and both blue and flathead catfish eat crustaceans and other fish, taking away the food supply that native carnivores like bluefish, rockfish, bass, flounder, croaker, shad, trout, and pretty much everything else that tastes good, also eats. We haven't yet figured out how to get the invasive catfish to eat the snakeheads and vice versa, but that would seem to solve our problem, wouldn't it?

Habitat restoration is another important factor in keeping the Bay's various fauna healthy. And oysters aren't the only creatures that benefit from artificial reefs, so do rockfish, bluefish, flounders, perch, and drum.

The first permitted artificial reef was put down in the Hollicutt's Noose area of Queen Anne's County back in the mid-1960s; currently there are twenty sites up and down the Bay. To fund these reefs, the Maryland Artificial Reef Initiative (MARI) was formed. With the funds collected by MARI, a volunteer, non-profit organization, various reef construction materials can be purchased and placed in the water. Among the materials permitted by the U.S. Army Corps of Engineers are sunken ships and barges, and even old tires. Portions of the original Woodrow Wilson Bridge, demolished in 2006, have been used as artificial reef. While it doesn't seem that dumping gigantic slabs of concrete in the water would do anything particularly helpful, the mere fact that it serves as a hard substrate raised above the silt-covered bottom is enough to attract bottom-dwelling creatures to attach themselves to it. And as we know, the more creatures that can filter and clean the water, the better.

Despite all the controversy surrounding the most appropriate ways to improve the Chesapeake Bay, it's safe to say that a multi-front war is being waged to reduce pollution and repopulate the estuary with species that make the ecosystem work. No one is satisfied with the state of the Bay as it exists right now, but after 400 years of abuse, no one said that fixing the problems would be a day at the beach either. We ended the last century with an awareness that much had to be done. So far in the twenty-first century, we have taken giant steps toward getting things done. The key to the future is vigilance.

Recipe Index

Bibliography

"About SMADC: The Tobacco Buyout," Southern MD Agricultural Development Commission, http://smadc.com/aboutsmadc/buyout.html.

"Air Pollution," Chesapeake Bay Program, http://www.chesapeakebay.net/issues/issue/air_pollution#inline.

"American Indians, Colonists Had Healthy Appetite for Crabs, Study Shows," Smithsonian Science News, accessed March 30, 2015, http://smithsonianscience.org/2015/02/american-indians-colonists-healthy-appetite-crabs-study-shows/.

Apple, R.W. Jr, "Sweet Corn That's Best With a Grain of Salt," *The New York Times,* August 25, 2004, http://www.nytimes.com/2004/08/25/dining/sweet-corn-that-s-best-with-a-grain-of-salt.html.

Baker, Mary Lou, *Seafood Lover's Chesapeake Bay: Restaurants, Markets, Recipes & Traditions.* First edition. Guilford, Connecticut: Globe Pequot Press, 2014.

Blake, Allison. *Explorer's Guide Chesapeake Bay: A Great Destination.* Sixth edition. Woodstock, Vermont: Countryman Press, 2005.

Blankenship, Karl, "Hatchery Spawns Hope for Crab Stock Enhancement." *Bay Journal,* September 1, 2005, http://www.bayjournal.com/article/hatchery_spawns_hope_for_crab_stock_enhancement.

Bready, James H, "Maryland Rye: A Whiskey the Nation Long Fancied—But Now Has Let Vanish." pp. 345-378 *Maryland Historical Magazine,* Winter 1990.

Brennessel, Barbara. *Diamonds in the Marsh: A Natural History of the Diamondback Terrapin.* Lebanon, New Hampshire: University Press of New England, 2006.

Brown, Travis H, "When It Rains, It Pours Tax Dollars in Maryland." *Forbes Magazine,* January 3, 2014, http://www.forbes.com/sites/travisbrown/2014/01/03/when-it-rains-it-pours-tax-dollars-in-maryland/.

Bureau of Industrial Statistics of Maryland, *Annual Report of the Bureau of Industrial Statistics of Maryland.* The Bureau, 1900.

Casey, Jim, "A Short History of Commercial Fishing in the Chesapeake

Region." http://dnr2.maryland.gov/fisheries/Documents/history_of_comm_fishing.pdf.

Chesapeake Bay Foundation, "EPA: Maryland Mostly on Track to Cleaner Water, but Some Problems Persist," June 12, 2015, http://www.cbf.org/news-media/newsroom/2015/06/12/epa-maryland-mostly-on-track-to-cleaner-water-but-some-problems-persist?srctid=1&erid=41844602&trid=b5ab2a21-409d-4ad4-b76a-48a53ed08af6.

Chesapeake Bay Foundation, "More Than Just the Bay: Creatures of the Chesapeake, American Shad," accessed June 15, 2015, http://www.cbf.org/about-the-bay/more-than-just-the-bay/creatures-of-the-chesapeake/american-shad.

Chesapeake Bay Foundation, "What Is the Chesapeake Bay Clean Water Blueprint." http://www.cbf.org/how-we-save-the-bay/chesapeake-clean-water-blueprint/what-is-the-chesapeake-clean-water-blueprint.

Cofield, Ron. "How the Hoe Cake (Most Likely) Got Its Name." *Historic London Town and Gardens,* May 2008.

Coulborne, E. "The History of the Strawberry Industry." Somerset Strawberry Festival. *http://www.somersetmdstrawberryfestival.com/the-history-of-the-strawberry-industry.*

Dewar, Heather, "Black Watermen Sail into View." *The Baltimore Sun,* February 8, 1999, http://articles.baltimoresun.com/1999-02-08/news/9902080017_1_leggett-chesapeake-bay-unsung-heroes.

Edwards, Scott, "Chesapeake Bay: An Open Toilet." Chesapeake Bay Action Plan, accessed January 27, 2015, http://www.bayactionplan.com/chesapeake-bay-open-toilet/.

Fahrenthold, David A., "Oyster-Saving Efforts a Wash in Chesapeake." *The Washington Post,* June 2, 2008. http://www.washingtonpost.com/wp-dyn/content/article/2008/06/01/AR2008060102499.html?hpid=moreheadlines.

"Fishy Research Leads to the Plight of the Blue Crab." *Washington Examiner,* November 2008, http://www.washingtonexaminer.com/fishy-research-leads-to-the-plight-of-the-blue-crab/article/26662.

Foley, Joan. *The Chesapeake Bay Fish and Fowl Cookbook: A Collection of Old and New Recipes from Maryland's Eastern Shore.* New York: Macmillan Publishing Co., 1981.

Ford, Ben, "Wooden Shipbuilding in Maryland Prior to the Mid-Nineteenth Century." http://www.academia.edu/2284534/Wooden_Shipbuilding_in_Maryland_Prior_to_the_Mid-Nineteenth_Century.

Giles, Dorothy. *Singing Valleys; the Story of Corn.* New York: Random House, 1940. Free Download & Streaming, accessed June 15, 2015. https://archive.org/details/singingvalleysst00gilerich.

Goodman, Peter S., "An Unsavory Byproduct: Runoff and Pollution." *The Washington Post,* August 1, 1999, http://www.washingtonpost.com/wp-srv/local/daily/aug99/chicken1.htm.

Gottlieb, Sara J. and Mona E. Schweighofer. "Oysters and the Chesapeake Bay Ecosystem: A Case for Exotic Species Introduction to Improve Environmental Quality?" *Estuaries* 19, no. 3 (September 1, 1996): 639–50. doi:10.2307/1352524.

Grescoes, Taras. "How to Handle an Invasive Species: Eat It." *The New York Times.* February 20, 2008, http://www.nytimes.com/2008/02/20/opinion/20grescoe.html?pagewanted=print&_r=0

Grumet, Robert S. Bay. *Plain, and Piedmont: A Landscape History of the Chesapeake Heartland from 1.3 Billion Years Ago to 2000.* Washington, D.C.: National Park Service Chesapeake Bay Program, 2000.

Hagy, James D. et al., "Hypoxia in Chesapeake Bay, 1950-2001: Long-Term Change in Relation to Nutrient Loading and River Flow." *Estuaries* 27, no. 4 (August 1, 2004): 634–58.

Halvorson, Aimee D., "Recent Additions of Warmwater Fish Species to Chesapeake Bay." *Northeastern Naturalist* 14, no. 4 (January 1, 2007): 651–56.

Holden, Constance, "Chesapeake Bay." *Science, New Series,* 172, no. 3985 (May 21, 1971): 825–27.

Hollier, Dennis, "Tasty Mutants: The Invention of the Modern Oyster." *The Atlantic,* September 29, 2014, http://www.theatlantic.com/technology/archive/2014/09/todays-oysters-are-mutants/380858/.

"How To Buy Direct." LocalCatch.org. http://www.localcatch.org/how-to-buy-direct/.

Imbriani, Kathy, "Home Guides: How to Grow Silver Queen Corn." SF Gate, http://homeguides.sfgate.com/grow-silver-queen-corn-45802.html.

Lewis Andrews, and J. Reaney Kelley. *Maryland's Way: The Hammond-Harwood House Cookbook.* First edition. Annapolis, Maryland: Hammond-Harwood House, 1966.

Maryland Department of Planning, Jefferson Patterson Park and Museum, "Maryland's Environment: A 20,000 Year History of Change." Maryland Dept. of Planning. Jefferson Patterson Park & Museum, http://www.jefpat.org/archeobotany/PDF/PaleobotEssay.pdf.

Maryland Historical Society Library Department, "Home-Made Wines Made of Dandelions": Prohibition in Maryland." *Underbelly,* February 20, 2014, http://www.mdhs.org/underbelly/2014/02/20/home-made-wines-made-of-dandelions-prohibition-in-maryland/.

May, Robert. *The Accomplisht Cook or, the Art & Mystery of Cookery.* London: Printed for Obaiah Blagrave at the Bear and Star in St Pauls Church-Yard, 1685.

McLenachan, Loren et al. "Do Community Supported Fisheries (CSFs) Improve Sustainability?" *Fisheries Research* 157 (September 2014): 62–69.

Mencken, H.L., *The Vintage Mencken,* compiler Alastair Cook. Reissue edition. New York: Vintage, 1990.

Miss Tyson. *Queen of the Kitchen: A Collection of "Old Maryland" Family Receipts for Cooking.* Philadelphia: T.B. Peterson and Brothers, 1874.

"New Study Says Chicken Manure Runoff Too Much For Chesapeake Bay," *CBS Baltimore,* accessed January 27, 2015, http://baltimore.cbslocal.com/2011/12/28/new-study-says-chicken-manure-runoff-too-much-for-chesapeake-bay/.

O'Brien, Dawn, and Rebecca Schenck. *Maryland's Historic Restaurants and Their Recipes.* Revised edition. Winston-Salem, N.C: John F. Blair Publisher, 1996.

Pfitzenmeyer, Hayes T. "Molluscs of the Chesapeake Bay." *Chesapeake Science* 13 (December 1, 1972): S107–15. doi:10.2307/1350662.

Russell, Marc J. et al., "Net Anthropogenic Phosphorus Inputs: Spatial and Temporal Variability in the Chesapeake Bay Region." *Biogeochemistry* 88, no. 3 (May 1, 2008): 285–304.

"Secrets from the Hoover Kitchen." *Galveston Daily News,* March 23, 1929.

Sheir, Rebecca. "Move Over, Smith Island Cake: Maryland's Unsung Culinary Delights." WAMU 88.5, accessed March 30, 2015, http://wamu.org/programs/metro_connection/14/07/25/move_over_smith_island_cake_marylands_unsung_culinary_delights.

Shields, John. *Chesapeake Bay Cooking: The Companion Cookbook to the Public Television Series*. First edition. New York: Broadway Books, 1998.

Shields, John, and Jed Kirschbaum. *Chesapeake Bay Cookbook: Rediscovering the Pleasures of a Great Regional Cuisine*. Reading, Mass.: Addison-Wesley, 1991.

Simmons, Melody. "Island's Past and Future, in a Layer Cake." *The New York Times*, March 31, 2008, http://www.nytimes.com/2008/03/31/us/31cake.html.

Stieff, Frederick Philip. *Eat, Drink, and Be Merry in Maryland*. Baltimore: Johns Hopkins University Press, 1997.

Stoll, Joshua S., Bradford A. Dubick, and Lisa M. Campbell. "Local Seafood: Rethinking the Direct Marketing Paradigm." *Ecology and Society* 20(2): 40 (2015). http://dx.doi.org/10.5751/ES-07686-200240.

The Pew Environment Group. "Big Chicken: Pollution and Industrial Poultry Production in America." *The Pew Environment Group*, July 27, 2011.

Wallach, Jennifer Jensen. *How America Eats: A Social History of U.S. Food and Culture*. Lanham, Maryland: Rowman & Littlefield, 2013.

Warner, William W. and John Barth. *Beautiful Swimmers: Watermen, Crabs and the Chesapeake Bay*. Reprint edition. Boston: Back Bay Books, 1994.

Wennersten, John R. *Maryland's Eastern Shore: A Journey in Time and Place*. First edition. Centreville, Maryland: Tidewater Publishing, 1992.

Wheeler, Timothy B., "Watermen Win Changes to Oyster Reef Restoration," *Baltimoresun.com*, accessed May 28, 2015, http://www.baltimoresun.com/features/green/blog/bs-md-oyster-restoration-20150523-story.html.

Zohar, Yonathan. "The Chesapeake Bay Blue Crab (*Callinectes Sapidus*): A Multidisciplinary Approach to Responsible Stock Replenishment." *Fisheries Science* 16 (2008): 24–34. doi:10.1080/10641260701681623.

Index